Winning Duplicate Tactics

DAVID B

Master Point Press • Toronto, Canada

Master Point Press
331 Douglas Ave.
Toronto, Ontario, Canada
M5M 1H2 (416)781-0351
Email: info@masterpointpress.com

www.masterpointpress.com
www.teachbridge.com
www.bridgeblogging.com
www.ebooksbridge.com

Library and Archives Canada Cataloguing in Publication
Bird, David, 1946-, author
        Winning duplicate tactics / David Bird.

Issued in print and electronic formats.
ISBN 978-1-77140-017-6 (pbk.).--ISBN 978-1-55494-609-9 (pdf).--
ISBN 978-1-55494-654-9 (epub).--ISBN 978-1-77140-803-5 (html)

        1. Duplicate contract bridge. I. Title.

GV1282.8.D86B57 2014   795.41'5   C2014-906124-2
                                                C2014-906125-0

Editor   Ray Lee
Cover and interior design   Olena S. Sullivan/New Mediatrix
Copyeditor   Marion Hoffmann
Interior format   Sally Sparrow

1 2 3 4 5 6 7   18 17 16 15 14
Printed in Canada

FOREWORD

Do you remember the first time you played in a duplicate pairs event? Someone, maybe a more experienced partner, explained to you about moving from table to table, filling in the scoresheet and ('It probably won't happen, don't worry') calling the Director. Yes, but what were you told about how to bid, play and defend in a duplicate pairs? In my case, it was nothing at all. It's true that you can get by if you play exactly the same way as you would in a home social game or an IMPs match. Duplicate pairs is a highly competitive game, though, and few contestants are happy just to 'get by'. They want to win — not just once in a while but regularly!

To be successful at duplicate pairs, you must adjust your bidding. You must know when to compete vigorously, taking a risk in doing so. You must also know when it is right to bid conservatively. You have to understand which contract to choose in various situations. In the play and defense you will meet similar dilemmas. Should you risk the contract for a lucrative overtrick? Should you risk giving away an extra trick in defense, hoping that you can beat the contract? These are some of the many topics that will be covered. I enjoyed writing this book and I hope you enjoy reading it!

CONTENTS

INTRODUCTION

We will start by looking at the scoring used for both IMPs and match-points. If you are already familiar with this, feel free to skip to page 13!

The scoring at IMPs

In an IMPs match between two teams, each deal is played twice and the scores are compared. Let's suppose that at the first table, South for Team A makes a vulnerable 4♠ contract to score +620. He will make this entry on his scorecard:

Team A   N-S scorecard

Board	Contract	By	Tricks	Score	IMPs
1	4♠	S	10	620	

The entry for the E-W pair at this table will be the same, except that they will enter the 620 in the minus column under 'Score.'

The deal will subsequently be replayed at the other table with the teams rotated by ninety degrees. So, Team B will now have the opportunity to take the N-S cards and match this result. For the purposes of this example, we will assume that their N-S pair bid more cautiously and stop in 2♠, making ten tricks but scoring only +170.

When all the boards in a set have been played, the two teams will reconvene to compare scores. Team A will find that they have gained +450 aggregate points on Board 1 and will convert this into IMPs (international match points). This is the conversion table:

Point Difference	IMPs	Point Difference	IMPs
20–40	1	750–890	13
50–80	2	900–1090	14
90–120	3	1100–1290	15
130–160	4	1300–1490	16
170–210	5	1500–1740	17
220–260	6	1750–1990	18
270–310	7	2000–2240	19
320–360	8	2250–2490	20
370–420	9	2500–2990	21
430–490	10	3000–3490	22
500–590	11	3500–3990	23
600–740	12	4000+	24

The present deal will result in a swing of 10 IMPs to Team A. Their N-S pair will add a 10 to the IMPs plus column:

Team A   N-S scorecard

Board	Contract	By	Tricks	Score	IMPs
1	4♠	S	10	620	10

The plus and minus IMPs will be added for the boards in this set (usually eight) to determine the current match score. Perhaps it will be 21-7 to Team A.

The main point to note is that the size of the difference in aggregate scores (450 here) makes a big difference. A large swing gives you more IMPs.

The scoring at matchpoint pairs

In a typical duplicate session at a bridge club, you enter as a pair with your partner. Each board will be played many times and your result will be compared with those of every other pair holding your cards at the other tables. You will score 1 MP (matchpoint) for every pair that you manage to beat. You will score 0.5 MPs for each pair who ties with your score. (Outside North America: you score 2 MPs for a win, 1 MP for a tie.)

Suppose that on Board 1 you play in 2♠ and make nine tricks for +140. On your personal scorecard, you will make the same entry that you would have done in an IMPs match:

Pair 5   *Scorecard*

Board	Contract	By	Tricks	Score	IMPs
1	2♠	S	9	140	

The North player will make a similar entry on a scoresheet associated with each board. At the end of the event, the scoring will be performed by the organizers. This might be the scoresheet for Board 1:

N-S	E-W	Contract	By	Tricks	N-S score	E-W score	N-S MPs	E-W MPs
1	5	2♠	S	9	140		3.5	1.5
2	4	2NT	N	9	150		5	0
3	2	4♠	S	9		50	0	5
4	1	3◇	E	7	100		1	4
5	6	2♠	S	9	140		3.5	1.5
6	3	2♠	S	8	110		2	3

For your +140 you scored 3.5 MPs out of a possible top score of 5 MPs, above average. Pair 4 N-S scored +100 for beating 3◇ by two tricks. This gave them only 1 MP. Had they ventured a penalty double and scored +300, they would have scored a 'top' of 5 MPs.

As you see, **the size of a score difference does not matter at all**. Even if you score only 10 aggregate points more than another pair, you beat them. The MP scores for all the boards will be added up and the winners announced.

PART ONE

BIDDING TACTICS

1

Making an Overcall

In this chapter we will take a close look at overcalls. When playing IMPs, you must consider the possible loss of a big penalty if your overcall is doubled. If you've bid on a poor suit and a defender sits over you with a strong trump holding, you may lose 500 or more when the opponents had nothing much their way. (Since a double by the next player will usually be for takeout, the penalty is more likely to arise after a reopening double by the opener.)

The situation is different at matchpoints. The occasional big penalty, when your luck runs out, is only one bad board. The size of the loss in aggregate points is irrelevant. If making such an overcall will improve your matchpoint score in the long run, you must go ahead and take the risk.

What is the purpose of an overcall?

What are the main aims of an overcall? Take a moment to think of your own answers before you read this list:

- to suggest a good opening lead to partner
- to allow your side to compete in a partscore auction
- to remove bidding space from the opponents
- to prepare the way for a good game contract or sacrifice

In general, you need at least a five-card suit to overcall at the one-level. When you bid at the two-level, you prefer to hold a six-card suit. Well, that is what the textbooks say. It has to be admitted that if you watch top players on the Internet, they will quite often make a two-level overcall on a good five-card suit. That's because they are unwilling to give the opponents an uncontested ride to their best contract.

How many points do you need for an overcall? At the one-level, you can be well short of the values needed for an opening bid. Suppose you hold ♠AQJ83 and little else. You would be reluctant to pass over an opponent's one-bid in a suit. When you make a non-jump overcall at the two-level (for example, 2◇ over 1♠), the risk of conceding a penalty is greater. Your point count tends to be not far short of that needed for an opening bid.

Should I overcall or double?

Way back in the mists of time, many players thought of an overcall as a weak intervention, based on a hand that generally contained less than the values for an opening bid. 'With a good hand, I would start with a double,' they would say.

This method was quite rightly abandoned. Nowadays a one-level overcall can be made on a weak hand or perhaps one with 17 points or so. The general guideline is that you overcall when you have a good suit and are happy to choose trumps; you prefer a takeout double when you wish to consult partner on the matter.

Suppose your right-hand opponent (RHO) opens 1◇ and you hold one of these hands:

(a)	(b)	(c)
♠ A Q 10 7 6	♠ A K J 8 7	♠ A K Q 6 4
♡ 10 7 4	♡ A 9 2	♡ K 9 7
◇ 8 2	◇ 4	◇ J 3
♣ Q 10 7	♣ K J 7 3	♣ A Q 10

On (a) you are happy to overcall 1♠ at any score. On (b) nearly all experts nowadays overcall 1♠ rather than start with a double. If your LHO raises to 2◇ and two passes follow, you can continue with a (takeout) double on the second round. Only when you are as strong as hand (c) will players reckon, 'That's too good for 1♠. I'd better start with a double.'

Weak jump overcalls

Since an overcall at the minimum level can be based on a strong hand, nowadays most pairs play 'weak jump overcalls'. In principle, such bids show a six-card suit and less than the values for an opening bid. They are preemptive in nature. That said, you should have reasonable playing strength when vulnerable, particularly if you are bidding at the three-level.

Suppose you are second to speak and the player on your right opens 1◇. What would you say on the following hands?

(a) ♠ A Q J 7 6 2
    ♡ 10 7
    ◇ 8 2
    ♣ J 10 7

(b) ♠ 9
    ♡ Q J 4
    ◇ 10 5 3
    ♣ K Q J 10 7 3

(c) ♠ K Q J 9 4
    ♡ 9 7
    ◇ J 9 7 2
    ♣ 10 4

Hand (a) is ideal for a 2♠ overcall at any score. With (b) you would bid 3♣ when non-vulnerable. Some would risk 3♣ vulnerable at matchpoints, but it is not to everyone's taste. Hand (c) is ideal for preemption and if you are non-vulnerable you would consider bidding 2♠, even though you hold only a five-card suit. Vulnerable, you would bid 1♠. You would not think of passing since it is essential to mention a suit of this quality.

Overcalling to suggest an opening lead

Even when you are almost certain that the opponents will be able to outbid you, an overcall may be valuable to suggest a good opening lead to partner. Look at this deal:

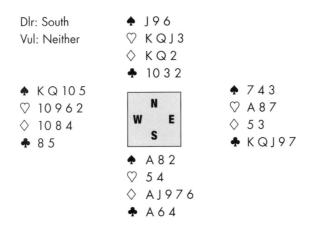

Dlr: South
Vul: Neither

North
♠ J 9 6
♡ K Q J 3
◇ K Q 2
♣ 10 3 2

West
♠ K Q 10 5
♡ 10 9 6 2
◇ 10 8 4
♣ 8 5

East
♠ 7 4 3
♡ A 8 7
◇ 5 3
♣ K Q J 9 7

South
♠ A 8 2
♡ 5 4
◇ A J 9 7 6
♣ A 6 4

West	North	East	South
			1◇
pass	1♡	2♣	pass
pass	dbl	pass	2NT
pass	3NT	all pass	

West leads the ♣8, prompted by East's overcall, and declarer has to go one down. Without the overcall West might well have led a spade.

When you are defending at matchpoints, you must work hard to prevent declarer scoring overtricks. Lead-directing overcalls therefore assume even greater importance. The best lead may not beat the contract, but if it converts a 650 into 620, this can be just as valuable. Of the four reasons to overcall, given earlier, lead direction becomes the most important.

Suppose your LHO opens 1♡ and his partner responds 2♣. In fourth seat you hold one of these hands:

(a) ♠ A K J 10 6 (b) ♠ A 8
    ♡ 8 3   ♡ K 5
    ◇ 10 4   ◇ J 10 9 7 6 2
    ♣ 9 7 6 2   ♣ K 6 5

You don't expect to win the auction on either hand, after the strong start to the opponents' sequence. At matchpoints, bid 2♠ on hand (a), ensuring a spade lead. Hand (b) has more playing strength but you should pass. Suppose your LHO ends up playing in 4♡. You don't want your partner to lead the ◇K from a doubleton.

At the one-level, particularly at matchpoints, you can consider overcalling on a chunky four-card suit. Here you deter the opponents from bidding a successful 3NT:

```
Dlr: South        ♠ 10 3 2         Matchpoints
Vul: Neither      ♡ A Q 8 5
                  ◇ A 10 7
                  ♣ K 6 4

♠ A K Q 7                          ♠ J 9 5
♡ 9 2            ┌─────────┐       ♡ J 10 6 4
◇ K 5 3         │    N    │       ◇ J 9 8 4 2
♣ 10 9 7 2      │ W     E │       ♣ 5
                │    S    │
                └─────────┘
                  ♠ 8 6 4
                  ♡ K 7 3
                  ◇ Q 6
                  ♣ A Q J 8 3
```

West	North	East	South
			1♣
1♠	dbl	pass	2♣
pass	2♠	pass	3♡
pass	4♡	all pass	

A 3NT game has nine top tricks, but it's difficult to reach once you over-call 1♠ on the West cards. Here N-S alight in 4♡, which requires a 3-3 trump break to have a chance. Unlucky!

Overcalling to remove bidding space

This deal arose in the semi-final of a big money tournament in Monte Carlo:

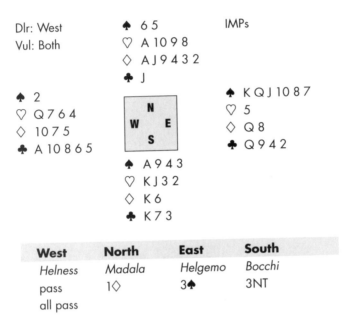

Dlr: West
Vul: Both

IMPs

♠ 6 5
♡ A 10 9 8
♢ A J 9 4 3 2
♣ J

♠ 2
♡ Q 7 6 4
♢ 10 7 5
♣ A 10 8 6 5

♠ K Q J 10 8 7
♡ 5
♢ Q 8
♣ Q 9 4 2

♠ A 9 4 3
♡ K J 3 2
♢ K 6
♣ K 7 3

West	North	East	South
Helness	Madala	Helgemo	Bocchi
pass	1♢	3♠	3NT
all pass			

A month before, these players had faced each other in the Bermuda Bowl final. Should Geir Helgemo bid 1♠, 2♠ or 3♠ on those East cards? Determined to take away as much bidding space as possible, Helgemo went all the way to 3♠. Norberto Bocchi very reasonably bid 3NT, which was passed out.

Tor Helness led the ♠2 to the ♠Q and South's ♠A. Bocchi cashed the ♢K and took a losing finesse of the ♢J. Five spades and five clubs later, he was seven down for −700.

At the other table, East overcalled only 2♠, leaving space for South to make a negative double. N-S found their heart fit and made eleven tricks for +650. The reward for Helgemo's 3♠ space-consuming overcall was a full 16 IMPs!

Responding to an overcall

When partner has overcalled and you have a trump fit, raise freely to consume bidding space. In general, you should be prepared to raise to the level indicated by your combined trump length. If the overcall is at the one-level, you expect partner to hold (at least) five trumps. When you hold four-card support and a bit of shape, you should be willing to raise to the three-level (nine trumps = a nine-trick contract.) If you go down, this will usually be in a good cause; the opponents could then have made a worthwhile contract their own way.

Suppose you are sitting West and the bidding has started like this:

West	North	East	South
	1◇	1♠	pass
?			

What would you bid on these West hands?

(a) ♠ K 10 6
    ♡ 10 8 4
    ◇ 9 6
    ♣ Q J 7 5 3

(b) ♠ A J 3
    ♡ K Q 9 2
    ◇ 10 7 6
    ♣ J 9 4

(c) ♠ K 10 6 4
    ♡ 7
    ◇ Q J 4 3
    ♣ 10 8 7 5

You raise to 2♠ on (a), removing a whole level of bidding space from North, who is likely to hold a good hand. Hand (b) could be described as a 'sound raise to the two-level.' You show this with a cue-bid of 2◇; if partner can rebid only 2♠, you will pass. On hand (c) you would bid 3♠. This is a preemptive raise, showing a four-card trump fit and some shape. Partner will not place you with a strong hand because you would then have cue-bid 2◇ instead.

Let's look at a full-deal example of the bidding following an overcall:

```
Dlr: East          ♠ J 5              Matchpoints
Vul: N-S           ♡ 10 8 5
                   ◇ Q 10 9 5
                   ♣ A Q 10 6

♠ K 10 8 6 2              N          ♠ A 9 7 4
♡ J                                  ♡ K 4 3
◇ K J 3 2          W         E       ◇ A 8 6
♣ J 3 2                  S           ♣ 9 7 4

                   ♠ Q 3
                   ♡ A Q 9 7 6 2
                   ◇ 7 4
                   ♣ K 8 5
```

West	North	East	South
		pass	1♡
1♠	2♡	3♡	pass
3♠	all pass		

A typical matchpoint partscore battle! West does not have much of a hand and is facing a passed partner. Nevertheless, he sees good reason to overcall. His side may find a playable spot in spades or push the opponents too high in their best fit. If East is fairly weak but has some spade support, there may be a profitable sacrifice in spades over a N-S game.

North raises to 2♡ and East has an excellent hand in support of spades. A raise to 3♠ would indicate a shapely hand with relatively few high-card points. Holding some top cards, East makes the more accurate bid of 3♡, a cuebid in the opponents' suit. If West were stronger he might then be able to bid a game. As it is, he signs off in 3♠.

The spade partscore goes one down (-50). This is a good score for E-W since South can make 3♡ (-140). The defenders can score the first four tricks against 3♡. A subsequent finesse of the ♡Q drops the ♡J offside and declarer returns to dummy to finesse against the ♡K.

- An overcall is multi-purpose. It can allow you to contest the auction, bid a good game or prepare for a sacrifice. It can also suggest a good opening lead or deprive the opponents of bidding space.

- A one-level overcall (1♠ over 1◇) may be based on a hand with a wide range of points (roughly about 8-17). A two-level overcall (2◇ over 1♠) is usually based on a hand with opening bid values.

- Most duplicate players use weak jump overcalls (2♡ over 1♣, for example). These are preemptive in intent. A jump overcall of 2♡ or 2♠ shows something close to a weak two opening.

- Overcall when you have a good suit and are happy to choose trumps. Prefer a takeout double when you have reasonable support for the unbid suits and wish to consult partner on the choice of a trump suit.

- At matchpoints, where overtricks rule the roost, lead direction is more important than at IMPs. When you have a borderline overcall, let the quality of your suit determine whether you bid or not.

- Any direct raise of an overcall is likely to be preemptive in nature. With a sound raise to some level, you begin with a bid in the opponent's suit.

TEST YOURSELF

Assume you are playing matchpoint pairs on the following problems.

1. Neither side is vulnerable and your RHO opens 1♣. What call will you make on each of these hands? Would you choose differently when vulnerable?

(a) ♠ K 6	(b) ♠ A J 4	(c) ♠ A K Q 9	(d) ♠ A K J 9 6
♡ J 7 3	♡ K Q 8 4 3	♡ A 2	♡ 8 3
◇ A Q 9 6 5 4	◇ Q 10 6 5	◇ 10 8 3	◇ J 10 7 3
♣ 9 2	♣ 7	♣ J 8 5 2	♣ 5 4

2. Only the opponents are vulnerable and your RHO opens 1◇. What call will you make on each of these hands?

(a) ♠ K Q 10 6 2	(b) ♠ A K J 10 4	(c) ♠ K 2	(d) ♠ J 5
♡ 10 7	♡ K 8 3	♡ 7 6	♡ A Q 10 9 5 2
◇ 8 3 2	◇ A	◇ 10 9 7 6	◇ 8 2
♣ Q J 5	♣ Q 9 6 2	♣ A K J 10 4	♣ J 9 3

3. Neither side is vulnerable. What action will you take as West when the bidding starts like this?

West	North	East	South
	1◇	1♡	pass
?			

(a) ♠ Q 7 6 2	(b) ♠ A 10 8 4	(c) ♠ 9 7 2	(d) ♠ J 10 9 3
♡ K J 7 2	♡ K Q 3	♡ 6	♡ A J 10 6 5
◇ 10 8 3 2	◇ 9 2	◇ Q 10 5	◇ 8
♣ 8	♣ J 10 6 2	♣ K J 10 9 7 6	♣ K J 4

4. Only your side is vulnerable. What action will you take as West when the bidding starts like this?

West	North	East	South
	1◇	1♡	2◇
?			

(a) ♠ 8 5 2	(b) ♠ 8 4	(c) ♠ A 10 7 6	(d) ♠ Q 3
♡ K 7 2	♡ A 8 7 3	♡ J 4	♡ A 5
◇ 8 4	◇ 10 9 2	◇ Q 10	◇ 9 7 6 2
♣ Q J 8 7 2	♣ A Q J 6	♣ K Q 10 7 6	♣ K J 8 5 3

1. On (a) bid 2◇ rather than 1◇. It is important to take away bidding space. With hand (b) prefer 1♡ to a double. If you double, you may miss a 5-3 heart fit. With hand (c) overcall 1♠. You want to enter the auction and cannot afford to double with only two hearts. On (d) try a 2♠ overcall when non-vulnerable, removing bidding space from your LHO. When vulnerable, or playing IMPs, it is more prudent to say just 1♠.

2. On (a) you overcall 1♠. Your hand is a minimum for a one-level overcall, but the suit is worth mentioning and it will inconvenience LHO if he holds a heart suit. If your suit was hearts instead of spades, you might still overcall, but it would be less attractive; you would not be taking away any bidding space. With (b) most players nowadays would start with 1♠. In this way you pick up the large number of occasions when partner has three-card spade support. If the opponents stop in 2◇, you plan to show your strength and support for the other suits with a second-round takeout double. Although you have only a five-card club suit on (c) you should overcall 2♣. This is always a tempting overcall to make over 1◇, because you cut out a one-level response in either major. Hand (d) is ideal for a weak-jump overcall of 2◇. Given the chance, you would have opened with a weak 2◇ bid. You would take all these actions at both matchpoints and IMPs.

3. With good four-card support and a side singleton on (a), you should raise preemptively to 3♡. Do not be one of those players who try to buy the contract in 2♡. North may then be able to rebid 3♣, allowing the opponents to discover a big club fit. Hand (b) represents a 'sound raise to the two-level'. You show this with a cuebid of 2◇. With (c) you should pass. A change-of-suit bid, such as 2♣, is constructive and shows not far short of opening bid values. (Some players treat a new suit as forcing.) If North doubles 1♡ for takeout and South leaves this double in, you can then rescue to 2♣. With (d) you go straight to 4♡. This will make life difficult for North if he holds some shapely hand of 18 points or so.

4. Hand (a) is fairly weak and a raise to 2♡ will consume no bidding space. Nevertheless, you should bid 2♡. By doing so, you will allow partner to compete further when he holds extra values. Hand (b) is a sound raise to the three-level and you should show this by cuebidding 3◊. A raise to 3♡ would show a weaker, more preemptive, type of hand. You are worth a bid on (c) but have no sound bid to make. On a hand of this type, you use a competitive double. This suggests the two unbid suits and doubleton support for partner's hearts. Hand (d) is awkward and there is no accurate call to make. A competitive double would be unwise with only two spades. You do best to raise to 2♡, rather than to sell out to their 2◊.

2

TACTICS WHEN BIDDING GAMES

In Chapter 6 we will consider how you should choose the right game (for example, 3NT or 4♡). Here we will look at how good a game needs to be before it is worth bidding.

Bidding a vulnerable game at IMPs

What odds do you need to bid a vulnerable game when playing IMPs? Although you can never calculate the odds precisely when you are looking at just one hand, let's suppose for the moment that the bidding has started 1♠-3♠ and you have to decide whether to bid 4♠. If you can make the spade game, you will score +620 instead of +170. That's a gain of 450 points. If you go one down in game, you will score −100 instead of +140, a loss of only 240 points. In terms of IMPs, you stand to gain 10 IMPs against losing 6 IMPs. You have much more to gain than to lose. If you think the game will have a 50% chance of success, bidding it is an easy decision.

As you would expect, it is actually worth bidding some games that are well short of a 50% chance.

You should bid a vulnerable game at IMPs if you judge that it will make 40% of the time or more.

What does a 40% game look like? This is an example:

West	East
♠ A K 8 6 4	♠ 9 7 5 2
♡ A 7 3	♡ K Q J 5
◇ J 9 5	◇ 6 4 3
♣ A Q	♣ 9 8

You can discard the ♣Q on the hearts, so to make the game you will need a 2-2 spade break (40%). Actually, you can add a bit because if the defenders don't cash their diamonds, you may survive a 3-1 trump break.

(You would hope to ditch a diamond on the fourth heart — whether or not the defender ruffs the fourth round with his master trump — and then take a successful club finesse.)

Bidding a non-vulnerable game at IMPs

When you are non-vulnerable, the game bonus is only 300. If you bid game and make it, you will score +420 instead of +170, a gain of +250 and a swing of 6 IMPs. If you bid game and go one down, you will score −50 instead of +140, a difference of −190 and a loss of 5 IMPs.

You should bid a non-vulnerable game at IMPs if you judge that it will make 50% of the time or more.

So, when non-vulnerable you should (in theory) not bid game on the E-W hands that we saw on the previous page. These cards just about merit a game contract:

West	East
♠ K J 6	♠ Q 7 5
♡ K Q J 7 6	♡ A 9 5 2
◇ Q 3	◇ 8 6 4 2
♣ A Q 2	♣ 6 3

You have three top losers and will need the club finesse to succeed unless North leads from the ♣K at Trick 1. The bidding will probably start 1♡-2♡ and West must then judge his next move. Looking at both hands, we can see that the game is a 50-50 shot.

When you are looking at only the West hand, life is not so clear-cut. Much will depend on how well the two hands fit. Here East has only 6 points but the ♠Q75 fits splendidly with West's ♠KJ6. West's ◇Q is of no value, as was quite likely. Bidding is not an exact science, as many painful memories remind us. West can hardly pass a single raise with 18 HCPs but, non-vulnerable at IMPs he is worth only a game try rather than a direct raise to 4♡.

Bidding a game at matchpoints

Everything is much simpler when you're playing matchpoint pairs. Whether you are vulnerable or not, you should bid games that are better than a 50% prospect. You are likely to gain half a top by bidding a making game; you will lose half a top by not bidding a making game.

Perhaps surprisingly, the potential gain and loss are not affected by how many other pairs bid the game.

```
Dlr: South        ♠ K 9 5          Matchpoints
Vul: Neither      ♡ J 9 7 6
                  ◇ 10 7 3
                  ♣ A 7 4
  ♠ 7 4 3                          ♠ 8
  ♡ Q 8 3         N                ♡ A K 10 2
  ◇ K Q J 4    W     E             ◇ 9 6 5 2
  ♣ K 5 2         S                ♣ 9 8 6 3
                  ♠ A Q J 10 6 2
                  ♡ 5 4
                  ◇ A 8
                  ♣ Q J 10
```

The bidding starts 1♠–2♠ and you can imagine that some pairs would then bid the spade game. It is roughly a 50% chance, depending on the club finesse. As you see, the ♣K is onside and those bidding the spade game will be rewarded.

In a six-table matchpoint pairs, with four of the six pairs bidding the game, this might be the scoresheet:

N-S	E-W	Contract	By	Tricks	N-S score	E-W score	N-S MPs	E-W MPs
1	5	4♠	S	10	620		3.5	1.5
2	4	4♠	S	10	620		3.5	1.5
3	2	4♠	S	10	620		3.5	1.5
4	1	3♠	S	10	170		0.5	4.5
5	6	4♠	S	10	620		3.5	1.5
6	3	2♠	S	10	170		0.5	4.5

Suppose N-S Pair 4 had decided to bid the successful game, instead of stopping in 3♠. All five pairs bidding the game would then have scored 3 MPs, their opponents scoring 2 MPs. N-S Pair 4 would have scored 3 MPs instead of 0.5, an increase of half a top.

Next we will say that the deal arises in a club where the players' bidding is more conservative. Only one N-S pair is bold enough to bid game now and this is the eventual scoresheet:

N-S	E-W	Contract	By	Tricks	N-S score	E-W score	N-S MPs	E-W MPs
1	5	2♠	S	10	170		2	3
2	4	3♠	S	10	170		2	3
3	2	3♠	S	10	170		2	3
4	1	4♠	S	10	620		5	0
5	6	2♠	S	10	170		2	3
6	3	3♠	S	10	170		2	3

Once again, any pair who decided to bid the successful game, rather than stopping short, would gain exactly half a top. Their score would jump from 2 MPs to 4.5 MPs.

As you see, you will gain half a top by bidding a making game and lose half a top by stopping short. By bidding all games that have more than a 50% chance, you will gain matchpoints in the long run.

You should bid a game at matchpoints if you think it will make more than 50% of the time.

The difference between 1♠-2♠ and 1♠-3♠

When partner gives you a double raise in a major suit (1♠–3♠), you usually have a simple two-way decision: should you pass or bid 4♠? We have already noted that you should bid a vulnerable game at IMPs if you think the chance of success is more than about 40%. When non-vulnerable, or when playing matchpoints, you need a 50% chance or more.

The situation is more complicated after a single raise. You then have a third option, to make a game try. It is fashionable to say: 'I never use game tries because I don't want to end at the three-level. After 1♠-2♠ I either pass or bid 4♠.' There's not much sense in this approach. If 4♠ will be a good contract opposite an upper-range 2♠ response and against the odds when partner is lower-range, you should involve partner in the decision making. By using help-suit game tries (usually bidding your second longest suit, where you have some losers to be covered), you can assist partner in making a good decision.

> **THINK ABOUT...**
>
> *Suppose you have raised 1♠ to 2♠ and partner than makes a game try. Holding four-card trump support instead of three-card will be worth around a whole extra trick! You should look favorably on such hands.*

Should I make a game try?

Let's look again at the West hand mentioned on the first page of this chapter:

West	West	East
♠ A K 8 6 4	1♠	2♠
♡ A 7 3	?	
♢ J 9 5		
♣ A Q		

Will you pass, make a game try or bid 4♠? Passing is too cautious with 18 points. You should make a game try, at least. A computer simulation reveals that 4♠ will succeed 59% of the time; 3♠ will be made 88% of the time.

At matchpoints a game contract is worth bidding if the prospects are more than 50%. With this West hand the chance of 4♠ succeeding is 59%. Does this mean that the bidding should go 1♠–2♠–4♠? Not necessarily! You have the option of making a game try (here 3♢). When East is upper-range or has good help for you in diamonds, he will bid game anyway. The question you need to ask yourself is this:

Will game be worth bidding at matchpoints (more than a 50% chance) when partner turns down a game try?

In these enlightened days we do not have to guess the answer. We can run a computer simulation where East holds a raise to 2♠ but would not accept a game try of 3♢, allowing you to stop in 3♠. Software developed by Taf Anthias (as used in our books, *Winning Notrump Leads* and *Winning Suit Contract Leads*) gives these results from 5000 deals:

3♠ or 4♠ when partner declines a 3♢ game try?

Contract	Makes	Avg tricks	MPs	IMPs (V)	IMPs (NV)
3♠	82.7%	9.4	54.3%	–1.6	–0.4
4♠	43.7%	9.4	45.7%	+1.6	+0.4

At matchpoints, making a game try of 3♢ and passing a sign-off in 3♠ will give you 54.3% of matchpoints. It is the right action. It's different at IMPs, where a game bonus is at stake. Stopping in 3♠ after partner's sign-off would then cost you an average of 1.6 IMPs when vulnerable, 0.4 IMPs when non-vulnerable. It follows that there is no point in a game try at IMPs; you should bid 1♠–2♠–4♠.

Well, that's brilliant. We have a clear example of how you should vary your bidding according to the type of bridge being played.

By the way, do not think that average swings of 1.6 (or even 0.4) IMPs per board are small numbers. They are big! Suppose your partnership's bidding decisions gained you an average of half an IMP on every board. That would be 16 IMPs during a thirty-two-board match and we have not even come to the wonderful decisions you intend to make as declarer or in defense!

We will see one more example, a borderline game decision at notrump.

West	West	East
♠ K 9 2		1NT
♡ A 10 3	?	
◇ Q 8 7 3		
♣ 8 5 2		

Should you pass, make a game try, or raise to 3NT?

On a sample of 5000 deals that match this start to the auction, 3NT was successful 57% of the time. That's a similar number to the previous example and, once again, it does not necessarily mean that you should jump to the game contract (3NT here). You have the option of making a game try — bidding 2NT, via Stayman if you use a direct 2NT as a transfer response.

Let's run a second simulation where we restrict the East hand to 15 points, when he would decline the game invitation. 3NT will then succeed only 43% of the time and will not be worth bidding at matchpoints or non-vulnerable at IMPs. Perhaps you are thinking that on some of the deals where 3NT would go down, so would 2NT. We can check the situation by using the software that compares contracts of 2NT and 3NT on the 5000 deals where East holds only 15 points.

2NT or 3NT when partner declines a 2NT game try?

Contract	Makes	Avg tricks	MPs	IMPs (V)	IMPs (NV)
2NT	82.8%	8.4	54.3%	−1.4	−0.3
3NT	42.6%	8.4	44.6%	+1.4	+0.3

2NT is the better contract at matchpoints, when partner declines your game try. At IMPs, particularly when vulnerable, you want to be in game regardless, and should raise directly to 3NT.

- When you are playing IMPs, you should bid a vulnerable game that has about a 40% or higher chance of success. When you are non-vulnerable, bid games that you judge will have a 50% or higher chance of success.

- The vulnerability makes no difference when playing matchpoints. The only relevant factor is the relative chance of making the game and going down. You should bid games that seem to be a 50% or better prospect.

- When the bidding starts 1♠-2♠ (or 1♡-2♡), do not leap straight to game just because you think such a contract will be worth bidding in the long run. By making a game try, you can stop at the three-level when partner has a minimum (or ill-fitting) raise. This will improve your matchpoint scores on such deals.

Test Yourself

1. WEST

	West	North	East	South
♠ K Q 10 6 3	1♠	pass	2♠	pass
♡ A 5	?			
◇ 8 6				
♣ A J 6 3				

You are vulnerable. What do you estimate is the chance of making 4♠ after this start to the auction? What action, if any, will you take at (a) IMPs, (b) matchpoints?

Suppose you improve the clubs to (1a) ♣AQ63 or to (1b) ♣AK63. What actions would be appropriate then?

2. WEST

	West	North	East	South
♠ K 9 8 6 4	1♠	pass	3♠	pass
♡ 6 5	?			
◇ A Q 10 5				
♣ K 3				

What do you estimate is the chance of making 4♠ after this start to the auction? What action will you take at IMPs and at matchpoints? Does it vary with the vulnerability? .

3. WEST

	West	North	East	South
♠ A 8 7 2			1◇	pass
♡ Q 10 5	1♠	pass	3♠	pass
◇ 9 4	?			
♣ 10 9 5 3				

You are vulnerable. What do you estimate is the chance of making 4♠ after this start to the auction? What action will you take at (a) IMPs, (b) matchpoints?

4. WEST

	West	North	East	South
♠ A 9			1NT	pass
♡ J 10 3	?			
◇ 9 6 5				
♣ K 10 7 6 2				

You are vulnerable and facing a 15-17 point 1NT. What is the chance of making 3NT, would you say? What action, if any, will you take at (a) IMPs, (b) matchpoints?

1. A computer simulation says that the chance of making 4♠ is 30%. You should certainly pass at matchpoints, even though the prospect of success would be higher than 30% on those hands where partner would accept a game try. If you were behind in an IMPs match, it would be a reasonable gamble to bid 3♣ (or even 4♠) in an attempt to gain a swing.

    (a) Upgrade the clubs to business class (♣AQ63) and the chance of making 4♠ rises to 46%. In that case, you should bid the game at IMPs and make a 3♣ game try at matchpoints.

    (b) Upgrade the clubs to first-class (♣AK63) and the prospects of making 4♠ reach a lofty 58%. You should bid 4♠ at all forms of the game.

2. The chance of making 4♠ is 54%. If you were vulnerable at IMPs, needing only a 40% prospect to justify bidding on, you would have an easy decision. Playing matchpoints, or non-vulnerable at IMPs, you should still bid game. If you go down... don't complain too loudly!

3. You expect partner to hold a six-loser hand and around 16-17 HCPs. Your ♡Q is a dubious value and the low doubleton in partner's suit is not particularly helpful. The chance of making game is only 29%, well below that needed even for a vulnerable game at IMPs, and you should pass. Suppose you improve the West hand only slightly, replacing the ♡Q by the ♡K:

    ♠A872   ♡K105   ◇94   ♣10953

    Now, after 1◇-1♠-3♠, the chance of making 4♠ is 54%, a worthwhile prospect in all situations.

4. You hold 8 points and 5-3-3-2 shape, with two potentially useful tens. The chance of making 3NT opposite a 15-17 point 1NT is 51%. If you take the plunge and raise directly to 3NT, you expect to score 51% of the matchpoints against those players who pass 1NT. At IMPs you will gain 1.5 IMPs per board (vulnerable) and 0.4 (non-vulnerable).

Is that the end of the story? No, because you can improve your prospects by making a 2NT game try. When partner accepts, he will make 3NT considerably more often than 51% of the time, with a matching rise in your matchpoint and IMP scores. When you stop in 2NT, game prospects will be less than 50% and you will still gain against those in a failing 3NT, even if you go down. There is a cost, however. When partner spurns your game try and you play in 2NT, you may lose matchpoints and IMPs to those who are in 1NT!

The mathematics are complicated, but your best tactics are to make a game try on this type of hand, whether at matchpoints or IMPs.

3

CHOOSING THE RIGHT PARTSCORE

In this chapter we will see how you should choose between one partscore and another. At IMPs you should aim for the contract that is more likely to be made. At matchpoints, you must bear in mind that a successful partscore at a given level scores most highly at notrump, fairly well in a major suit and least well in a minor suit.

Should I show a five-card major opposite 1NT?

Partner opens 1NT and you hold a five-card major and at least enough for a game try. It is obvious to start with a transfer and then bid some number of notrump. Partner can then pass with a doubleton in your suit and can usually correct to your suit with three or more cards in support.

Now suppose your partner opens 1NT and you have a weak hand with a five-card major. You must decide whether to pass or transfer to the major, where partner may hold only doubleton support. What should you do? Let's look at an example and see what answer a computer simulation gives us. Partner opens a 15-17 point 1NT and you hold this hand as responder:

$$\spadesuit \ 10\,8\,6\,5\,2$$
$$\heartsuit \ J\,9$$
$$\diamondsuit \ Q\,8\,3$$
$$\clubsuit \ 9\,7\,3$$

Should you pass 1NT or make a 2♡ transfer bid? Does the answer differ, according to whether you are playing IMPs or matchpoints?

Your major suit is weak and probably impossible to establish and enjoy at notrump. Playing in 2♠ is surely advisable, since you are then more likely to score some spade tricks. Here are the computer simulation results:

Responding to 1NT with a weak five-card major & 3 HCP

Contract	Makes	Avg tricks	MPs	IMPs (V)	IMPs (NV)
1NT	14.9%	5.4	33.5%	−1.4	−1.0
2♠	26.3%	6.9	66.5%	+1.4	+1.0

It's a big win for playing in 2♠. Both contracts are very likely to fail, but you can expect to go one or two down in 1NT, only one down in 2♠.

Let's make the responding hand stronger with better spades:

♠ K J 6 5 2
♡ 8 7 5
◊ K 10 8
♣ 10 2

What now? Should you pass 1NT or make a 2♡ transfer bid?

Responding to 1NT with a strong five-card major & 7 HCP

Contract	Makes	Avg tricks	MPs	IMPs (V)	IMPs (NV)
1NT	87.3%	8.1	39.6%	−0.8	−0.7
2♠	91.1%	9.0	60.4%	+0.8	+0.7

Playing in 2♠ is still much better, although the margin has been reduced. That's because you may be able to score several spade tricks in notrump.

Should I give preference to the major suit?

At matchpoints, a major-suit partscore is likely to score more than one in a minor suit. Yes, but only if you make the contract! How do you view this bidding situation:

WEST	West	North	East	South
♠ K 2			1♠	pass
♡ Q 10 7 4	1NT	pass	2◊	pass
◊ 9 8 6 3	?			
♣ J 9 5				

Playing matchpoints, should you pass or correct to 2♠?

Your partner probably holds only five spades, along with four or five diamonds. If instead his shape was 6-4, he might decide to rebid the spades when playing matchpoints. We can say with some confidence that 2◇ is more likely to be made than 2♠, so that's the contract to choose at IMPs (although the opponents might not allow the bidding to die there). You need to judge whether 2♠ will give you more matchpoints over the long haul. Let's see what the computer simulation says:

Spades or diamonds after 1♠-1NT-2◇?

Contract	Makes	Avg tricks	MPs	IMPs (V)	IMPs (NV)
2◇	66.7%	8.1	71.6%	+2.5	+1.9
2♠	31.9%	7.0	28.4%	–2.5	–1.9

Not a close contest! It is miles better to stick with diamonds (at both matchpoints and IMPs).

Should I pass a 1NT response?

What is your reaction to this bidding situation?

WEST	West	North	East	South
♠ K Q 9 8 2	1♠	pass	1NT	pass
♡ J 6	?			
◇ A 9 7 2				
♣ K 5				

You are playing matchpoints and partner's 1NT is non-forcing. You can assume that he will hold around 6-10 points and will not have three-card spade support. Should you pass or rebid 2◇?

Many players rebid 2◇ without even considering any other action. Remember, though, that 1NT is an attractive contract. You know that there is no eight-card fit in spades and there may well be no 4-4 fit in diamonds.

A profile of 5000 deals fitting this start to the auction revealed some interesting information:

East's length in West's suits

	0	1	2	3	4	5	6+
♠	5%	30%	65%				
◇	0%	6%	20%	31%	26%	13%	4%

When you choose to rebid 2◇ and eventually play in a suit where you have only seven trumps (maybe six), you can expect to do worse than you would have done in 1NT. Even when you do find a diamond fit of eight cards or more (a 43% chance), you might have scored better in

1NT. Occasionally, partner will be able to bid 2♡ effectively over 2♢, but the chance of him holding six or more hearts is only 13%. If East plays in 1NT opposite this West hand, he will make the contract 53% of the time. Your best action is to pass 1NT.

What happens when your second suit is hearts?

WEST	West	North	East	South
♠ A Q 9 8 2	1♠	pass	1NT	pass
♡ K J 6 5	?			
◇ K 4				
♣ 10 7				

Playing IMPs, there is an incentive to rebid 2♡, since if partner has heart support you might be able to make game in the suit. You can risk the same rebid at matchpoints and are likely to improve your score when you find a heart fit (again a 43% chance). When there is no fit, particularly if partner holds something like 1=3=5=4 shape, you may wish you had stopped in 1NT. It's a close decision.

Should I pass a 1NT rebid?

When partner opens 1◇ or 1♣ and rebids 1NT, showing 12-14 points, it may not be obvious whether you should pass this or go to two of his minor, where you have a fit. What do you normally choose to do in this situation?

WEST	West	North	East	South
♠ K 10 8 4			1◇	pass
♡ K 5	1♠	pass	1NT	pass
◇ Q 9 7 2	?			
♣ 10 5 3				

Partner will hold four diamonds (maybe five). Eight tricks in 2◇ will match seven tricks in 1NT, giving you +90. If partner can score +120 for eight tricks in 1NT, you would need an unlikely ten tricks in diamonds to beat this with +130. What should you do?

We will start by looking at the computer simulation results for this particular West hand:

Diamonds or Notrump after 1◇-1♠-1NT?

Contract	Makes	Avg tricks	MPs	IMPs (V)	IMPs (NV)
1NT	56.0%	6.7	36.1%	−1.6	−1.2
2◇	80.0%	8.3	63.9%	+1.6	+1.2

It's a surprisingly big win for 2◇. This is due to the fact that 2◇ will be made much more often than 1NT. It is true to say that the opponents may not be willing to let the bidding die in 2◇ and will sometimes contest the auction.

Opening 1NT with 5-4-2-2 shape

When you hold 15-17 points and certain variations of 5-4-2-2 shape, it can work well to open 1NT — particularly at matchpoints, where this will usually be a great contract if passed out. Look at these three hands:

(a) ♠ Q 6
♡ A J 6 2
◇ K Q 8 5 4
♣ K 5

(b) ♠ K 3
♡ Q 10
◇ A J 7 6 2
♣ A J 5 4

(c) ♠ Q 9
♡ A J 8 7 2
◇ K Q 7 6
♣ A 10

Many players would open 1NT on (a). If you open 1◇ instead, you are not strong enough to reverse to 2♡ over 1♠ and would have to rebid 2◇ (possibly a 5-2 or 5-1 fit). On (b), after 1◇-1♡/1♠, you can show your four-card club suit conveniently, but this will bypass 1NT. It will work well in the long run to open 1NT instead. On (c) the odds change. You have a five-card major and partner will often hold three of the eight missing hearts. It is better to open 1♡.

Rebidding 1NT with a singleton

Although some players refuse to do it, you will fare well at matchpoints by rebidding 1NT on some hands that contain a singleton in partner's suit.

WEST	West	North	East	South
♠ 9	1◇	pass	1♠	pass
♡ A J 8 3	?			
◇ K J 7 6 5				
♣ K 10 4				

What would you rebid on this hand? You are not strong enough to rebid 2♡. If you make the traditional rebid of 2◇, you may play there when partner has only two diamonds (even one). A 1NT rebid is recommended.

Suppose next that you hold this hand, which does offer a sound alternative rebid:

WEST	West	North	East	South
♠ 9	1◇	pass	1♠	pass
♡ A 10 7	?			
◇ A Q 9 7 3				
♣ Q 9 8 4				

No one can criticize if you rebid 2♣ on this hand, but you will often end up playing in 2◇ on a 5-2 fit. You can expect to reap a greater harvest of matchpoints by rebidding 1NT.

Once you have added this maneuver to your bidding style, you must revisit this bidding situation:

WEST	West	North	East	South
♠ K 10 8 6 4			1◇	pass
♡ K 7 2	1♠	pass	1NT	pass
◇ J 9	?			
♣ Q 8 3				

Should you pass 1NT or rebid 2♠? Players have argued on this point for decades. Let's add one more opinion by running a 5000-deal simulation — assuming for the moment that East will never rebid 1NT with a singleton spade and will never raise to 2♠ with only three trumps. (These are the most favorable conditions for West to rebid 2♠.)

2♠ or pass, after 1◇–1♠–1NT?

Contract	Makes	Avg tricks	MPs	IMPs (V)	IMPs (NV)
1NT	79.8%	7.4	47.8%	–0.05	+0.03
2♠	73.9%	8.1	52.2%	+0.05	–0.03

It is almost a dead heat! There is nothing in it when playing IMPs and the smallest advantage for rebidding 2♠ at matchpoints.

I recommend you open 1◇ and raise 1♠ to 2♠ on a hand such as:

♠ A 9 4   ♡ Q 6   ◇ A 10 5 4 2   ♣ K 9 7

If your partnership is willing to do this then the odds switch in favor of passing a 1NT rebid. If your partnership is happy to rebid 1NT with a singleton in partner's suit, then passing 1NT becomes a big winning action.

- When partner opens 1NT and you have a weak hand with a five-card major, make a transfer response rather than passing. This applies at both IMPs and matchpoints.

- Playing partscores in a major suit rather than a minor suit will give you a better matchpoint score only when you make the contract. If the bidding starts 1♡/1♠–1NT;2♣/2♢, you should pass with two cards in the opener's major and four cards in his minor (unless you are strong enough for a raise).

- 1NT is a splendid contract to play at matchpoints (particularly when you are non-vulnerable). When in range, you should be willing to rebid 1NT with a singleton in partner's suit.

- When you hold 5-4-2-2 shape, with five cards in a minor suit and a four-card heart suit that is impractical to rebid, be prepared to open 1NT. At matchpoints, any hands with 5-4-2-2 shape, including a five-card minor, may fare well after a 1NT opening.

- Similarly, it is fine to rebid 1NT on a 12-14 point hand with some variations of 5-4-2-2 shape.

- After an auction such as 1♢–1♠–1NT, pass, rather than rebidding a five-card spade suit.

TEST YOURSELF

1. What is your matchpoint bidding plan on these three hands if partner responds 1♡ or 1♠ to your opening bid?

    (a) ♠ 6
        ♡ K 10 4
        ◇ A Q 10 6 2
        ♣ Q 10 7 3

    (b) ♠ A J 2
        ♡ J 4
        ◇ K 8 7 6 5 2
        ♣ K 7

    (c) ♠ 9 3
        ♡ K 2
        ◇ K J 8 7
        ♣ A Q 7 6 2

2. What is your matchpoint bidding plan on these three hands?

    (a) ♠ A
        ♡ K J 7
        ◇ Q 9 8 4
        ♣ A Q 10 6 2

    (b) ♠ K J 2
        ♡ A Q 10 7 3
        ◇ A 4
        ♣ Q 9 6

    (c) ♠ 9 3
        ♡ K Q 8 7 3
        ◇ J 9 4 2
        ♣ A Q

3. What will you do next, playing matchpoints, on this West hand?

West	West	East
♠ J 2		1♠
♡ Q J 7 4	1NT	2◇
◇ K 7 5	?	
♣ 9 6 5 2		

4. Still West and playing matchpoints, what will you do next here?

West	West	East
♠ K 10 7 4 2		1◇
♡ K 6 2	1♠	1NT
◇ 4	?	
♣ J 9 6 4		

ANSWERS

1.(a) You open 1◇. If partner responds 1♡, you should raise to 2♡. This will play well in a 4-3 fit if partner passes (he can take spade ruffs in your hand.) If partner is strong enough to advance, he can check whether you have four-card support. When the bidding starts 1◇-1♠, you should rebid 1NT, showing 12-14 points. There is a big chance that 1NT will be the most productive contract and you're the only guy who can bid it!

(b) Again you open 1◇. If partner responds 1♡, it is better to rebid 2◇ than 1NT (65.6% of the matchpoints against 34.4%, when partner passes). Players are willing to open 1NT on this shape (when in range), but that is partly because of the preemptive benefit. Once you open 1◇, you have a heavy expectation of a diamond fit on this auction (Partner will hold two diamonds with frequency 47%, three diamonds 28%.)

(c) You open 1♣. (Do not contemplate opening 1◇ on this shape, intending to rebid 2♣.) If partner responds 1♠, you can rebid 1NT. If instead partner responds 1♡, it is not very attractive to rebid 1NT with a low doubleton in spades. It is better to rebid 2♣.

2.(a) Suppose you open 1♣. You will have an awkward rebid when partner responds 1♠. You are not quite strong enough to reverse to 2◇ and a 1NT rebid would show 12-14 points. Best in the long run is to open 1NT on this hand type.

(b) If you open 1♡, you will not really know what to do when partner responds 1♠, 1NT, 2♣ or 2◇! It is easily best to open 1NT, despite holding a five-card major.

(c) Open 1♡. If partner responds 1♠, rebid 1NT rather than 2◇. If instead partner responds 1NT, you know that he will hold at most three spades and two hearts. There is quite a good chance of finding a 4-4 diamond fit and it is a close decision whether you should pass or rebid 2◇.

3. Partner might hold five diamonds, in which case you could be better off passing 2◇. The chance of making 2◇ is 47% compared with 41% for 2♠. However, 2♠ is easily the better matchpoint contract because you will score more when you manage to make the contract. At matchpoints, 2♠ will outscore 2◇ by 61% to 39%. You should therefore correct to 2♠.

4. You should pass 1NT. Playing the methods that are suggested in this chapter, partner might hold:

♠ 8   ♡ A Q 5 3   ◇ A Q 8 7 3   ♣ Q 10 5

A contract of 2♠ would then be hopeless. Also, see how well partner has done to rebid 1NT with his singleton spade. The alternative contract of 2◇ would have been a poor matchpoint spot.

4

PREEMPTIVE OPENINGS

The main purpose of a preemptive opening bid is to take away bidding space from your opponents, who may well have a good contract somewhere. When you have the chance to make such a bid, it is a losing tactic to look for an excuse to pass instead. Playing in an IMPs match, it is aggravating to miss a good contract or to get too high, because of an opponent's preempt. It is doubly annoying if you discover that your teammates did not make the same preempt and the pair holding your cards were able to sail into the best contract!

Weak two-bids

Playing matchpoints, it is essential that you can open on weak two types of hands. Suppose you pick up this collection:

♠ K Q J 8 7 2   ♡ 7 6 2   ◇ 8   ♣ 10 4 3

You are likely to score five tricks if you choose trumps, at most one if you defend a contract in some other suit. What does that tell you? It means that your hand is ideal for preemptive action. If you are playing weak two-bids, open 2♠ in any of the first three seats and at any vulnerability!

Don't be one of those players who say, 'I was too weak for a vulnerable weak two', or 'I didn't like to open 2♠ with four cards in the other major.' Put yourself in the place of your left-hand opponent, who may well hold a good hand. Do you think he will be happy to start the description of his hand with two rounds of bidding removed?

Even if you do occasionally get caught for an unpleasant penalty when vulnerable, it is only one bad matchpoint score. You will be amply compensated by many good scores when the opponents fail to reach their best contract.

Responding to a weak two-bid

Many players overbid in response to a weak two. If you play a fairly bold style of two-level openings, you must make some allowance for this when deciding how to respond. In general, you should bid freely when you have a fit, to make life awkward for the opponents. Without a fit, bid conservatively.

This is the standard method of responding to a weak two opening bid of 2♡:

2♠	invitational
2NT	game try
3♣/3♢	forcing and natural
3♡	preemptive raise, not invitational
3♠	forcing and natural
3NT	to play, may include a long minor
4♡	may be preemptive, may be strong.

How would you respond to a weak 2♡ when you hold one of these hands with trump support?

(a)	♠ 9 7 2	(b)	♠ 10 8	(c)	♠ A Q 8 7 2
	♡ K 10 4		♡ Q J 9 2		♡ K 9 7
	♢ 8 2		♢ K J 8 7 4		♢ 10 3
	♣ A J 9 7 3		♣ 7 3		♣ A Q 10

On (a) you can guess that the opponents have a good contract somewhere, maybe a game. Make it harder for them by raising preemptively to 3♡. On (b) you are almost certain that the opponents can make game in spades. Raise all the way to 4♡ to take away their bidding space. Holding (c), you mentally place partner with ♡AQJxxx and little more. Six heart tricks and two aces will bring the total to eight. You may make one or both black queens or set up the spades. Again, raise to 4♡ — this time with a constructive purpose.

Opening three-bids

When you preempt at the three-level, there is slightly more chance that the defenders will be able to catch you for a useful penalty. You should therefore use some discretion, particularly when you are vulnerable. The field is yours in the third seat, but preempts in the first and particularly the second seat should be sound when vulnerable.

Some of you may be as old as I am and remember being taught the Rule of 500 in your youth. This implied that your hand should be more or less good enough on its own to safeguard against a penalty of more than 500. This guideline has rightly been consigned to the mists of time. Firstly, it is not so likely that the opponents can catch you when nearly everyone plays takeout doubles. Secondly, hands that contain seven likely tricks when you are vulnerable are most unlikely to be weak enough for a preempt. You could wait for months, if not years, to be dealt such a hand.

Players nowadays realize that preempts are very effective and are willing to use them on a wide range of hands — particularly at matchpoints and particularly when non-vulnerable. Look at these hands:

(a)	♠ K Q J 9 8 7 2	(b)	♠ 8	(c)	♠ 9
	♡ 9 7 2		♡ 10 4		♡ A Q J 10 8 6 4
	◇ 8		◇ 7 6 2		◇ 10 7
	♣ 10 9		♣ K Q 8 6 4 3 2		♣ Q J 4

On (a) of course you want to preempt to the limit! Open 3♠ under any conditions. Do not chicken out and open with a weak 2♠. It is very much easier for the opponents to bid over a weak two than a weak three. Some guys who favor the fast lane would open 4♠.

Hand (b) is okay for a non-vulnerable 3♣. You would not open 3♣ when vulnerable, except perhaps in the third seat at matchpoints.

Hand (c) may satisfy the old-fashioned Rule of 500, but it is too strong for a three-bid even when vulnerable. Open 1♡ instead.

Responding to a three-level preempt

There are two reasons why you might raise a 3♡ or 3♠ preempt to game. Firstly, your hand is quite strong and you fancy the chance of partner making the game. Secondly, you have a good fit for partner's suit and you want to raise the preemptive bar one level higher.

Suppose partner opens 3♡ and you have to decide your response on one of these hands:

(a)	♠ A Q 8 7	(b)	♠ 10 7 2	(c)	♠ K 9
	♡ 9 7		♡ K 10 6 4		♡ 6
	◇ Q 10 6		◇ 9		◇ A Q 7
	♣ A K 10 3		♣ K J 9 7 4		♣ A K Q J 8 7 3

On (a) you would raise to 4♡. Nothing is certain in this life, but you would expect partner to make the contract when his preempt was a vulnerable one. If he was non-vulnerable, there would be more chance of 4♡ failing, but the game might still be a reasonable shot.

With hand (b) you would raise to 4♡ defensively. In other words, you expect to go down in 4♡, but the opponents can probably make game their way. By taking away a round of bidding, you hope to make it more difficult for the fourth player to bid, or perhaps find the best fit.

On (c) you respond 3NT. This does not show a balanced hand. When you hold a strong 1NT type of hand with two or three hearts, you are more likely to raise to 4♡. The 3NT response strongly suggests a long minor and your partner should not think of reverting to 4♡.

Opening four-bids

When you open 4♡ or 4♠, do not forget that such a bid is a preempt. You show a relatively weak hand with a long suit. If you make the mistake of opening at the four-level with something like 18 points, you risk missing a slam when partner has enough honors to fill in your gaps. Look at these three hands, supposing you are in the first or second seat:

(a)	♠	A Q J 9 8 7 5 2	(b)	♠	8	(c)	♠	A J 8 7 5 4 2
	♡	7 5		♡	A K Q J 8 6 3		♡	K Q 4
	◇	8		◇	K J 7 2		◇	8 6
	♣	Q 7		♣	6		♣	10

THINK ABOUT...

Some players use openings of 4♣ and 4◇ as Namyats (or South African Texas), showing a strong opening of 4♡ and 4♠ respectively. You might open 4♣ on:
♠97 ♡KQJ109853 ◇A4 ♣9 reserving 4♡ for weaker hands.

Hand (a) is perfect for 4♠. You will score lots of tricks if spades are trumps, hardly any if the opponents choose trumps. This is the test of whether your hand is suitable for a preemptive opening.

Hand (b) is too strong. Give partner just two aces and you are close to making a slam. Open 1♡ instead.

Hand (c) is unsuitable for 3♠ or 4♠. You are too strong for 3♠, and the suit is not good enough to bid 4♠. Easily best is to open 1♠, intending to rebid just 2♠ since you have so few points.

Preempting in the third seat

You will often hear players saying, 'Anything goes in the third seat!' What does that mean? Suppose you have a weak hand and the two players before you both pass. Your left-hand opponent is very likely to hold a good hand. It is only human nature to try to make life as difficult as possible for him. You can do this by preempting on a weaker hand than normal, particularly at matchpoints, and particularly when you are non-vulnerable.

Suppose you are third to speak after two passes and hold one of these not-very-special hands:

(a) ♠ Q 10 9 8 7 5 2   (b) ♠ 8   (c) ♠ K Q 7 6 2
    ♡ 7 5 3   ♡ J 9 6   ♡ 4 2
    ◇ J 6   ◇ 5 4 2   ◇ J 8 6 2
    ♣ 5   ♣ K Q J 7 6 2 ♣ 10 5

Non-vulnerable, you should not hesitate to open 3♠ on (a). Just imagine how aggravating this will be for the next player, who holds a great hand and is looking forward to impressing everyone with his wonderful bidding methods. Remember that nearly everyone uses a double for take-out, so there is little risk of ending up doubled.

It is automatic to open 3♣ on (b), non-vulnerable in the third seat. At matchpoints many would make the same bid in first or second seat too (also in the third seat with both vulnerable). You will score five tricks if you choose trumps, probably not a single trick if you defend. It is not just a question of shutting the next player out. Suppose he has a good major suit. He will either have to bid it at the three-level or pass. When he does bid, his partner may need to guess whether he holds 12 points or 18.

With (c) you open a matchpoint 2♠ at any score. You force the player in the fourth seat to bid at the three-level, and then his partner will often have to guess whether to raise.

You may also choose to preempt on stronger hands than you would in the first two seats. The risk of missing a game is minimized when partner is a passed hand. After two passes, you hold one of these hands:

(a) ♠ 2   (b) ♠ J 4   (c) ♠ 9 7 3
    ♡ K 6   ♡ 10 6 2   ♡ K Q J 10 4 2
    ◇ J 7 4   ◇ A K Q J 9 4 ◇ Q J 6
    ♣ A Q J 10 7 6 5 ♣ 10 3   ♣ 4

Open 3♣ on (a). The hand would be much too strong for a preempt in the first two seats. Even in the third seat it is possible that you might miss a playable 3NT by opening 3♣. It is many times more likely that your opening bid will inconvenience the opponent on your left.

Are you going to give the next player an easy ride by opening 1◇ on (b)? Open 3◇ and enhance your reputation as a difficult opponent. You have little defense on hand (c) and should open 3♡ rather than 2♡.

- Preempts work! Don't be one of those players who tends to find an excuse for not preempting. Create problems for your opponents.

- Preempts should be sound in the first and second seats. Your partner has not passed and you do not want to lose bidding space if he holds a strong hand.

- In the third seat, you may hold three different types of preempts: normal, very weak, or surprisingly strong. Let the opponents guess which type you hold. The important thing is to remove their bidding space and force them to guess what to do.

TᴇꜱT Yᴏᴜʀꜱᴇʟf

1. Neither side is vulnerable and you are playing matchpoints. What action would you take in first seat with these hands?

(a) ♠ K 10 8 7 6 2　(b) ♠ 7 2　　　(c) ♠ J 9 7 6　(d) ♠ J 9 7 6 5 2
　　♡ Q 10 4　　　　　♡ A Q 10 8 7 4　♡ K Q 9 8 5 2　♡ 10 6 4
　　♢ 6 5　　　　　　♢ 9 8 4　　　　♢ Q　　　　　♢ A K 7
　　♣ J 7　　　　　　♣ A 3　　　　　♣ 10 3　　　♣ 8

2. Only the opponents are vulnerable. It is matchpoints and you are in third seat with the previous two players passing. What action will you take?

(a) ♠ 8　　　　(b) ♠ K J 10 7 3　(c) ♠ 9 3　　　　(d) ♠ 9 7
　　♡ 9 6 2　　　　♡ 7 5 3　　　　♡ J 5　　　　　♡ A K Q 6
　　♢ J 10 5　　　♢ 10 9　　　　♢ A K Q 9 8 5　♢ 5
　　♣ K Q 10 7 6 2　♣ Q J 6　　　♣ 10 8 4　　　♣ J 9 7 6 4 2

3. Only your side is vulnerable and you are playing matchpoints. What action would you take in second seat with these hands?

(a) ♠ Q 8　　　　(b) ♠ K Q J 9 7 6　(c) ♠ 6　　　　(d) ♠ A Q 9 7 6 5
　　♡ K 9 7 6 5 3　　♡ 10 9 3　　　♡ J 4　　　　♡ K 10 9 4
　　♢ Q 7 4　　　　♢ A 8 4　　　　♢ 10 7 3　　　♢ J 4
　　♣ 8 2　　　　　♣ 5　　　　　　♣ A K Q 8 7 6 3　♣ 6

1.(a) You open 2♠. Of course you do! Don't be one of those players who says, 'I like to hold a better suit for a weak two.' Everyone loves to play against players who pass on this hand, giving them an easy time. Imagine how much more difficult it will be to bid when they have to start over 2♠.

(b) This hand is too strong for a weak two. Open 1♡.

(c) Some players would open 2♡, seizing any opportunity to preempt. It is better to pass in the long run, otherwise you may miss a good contract in spades. Look at it another way — you do not need to take a risk to shut out the spades when you hold four spades yourself.

(d) You have to draw the limit somewhere and your suit here is too weak for 2♠. Ideally, a preemptive opening should have good playing strength if the long suit is trumps and relatively few defensive tricks if the opponents choose trumps. Here your hand is the opposite. You have two defensive tricks outside and a feeble spade suit. (Yes, you will find players who do open 2♠!)

2.(a) You can expect the hand on your left to be strong, perhaps with length in the majors. Make life difficult for him by opening 3♣. Do not even think that this is a bit bold and daring. It is ordinary bridge! Nearly everyone plays that a double is for takeout, so you are very unlikely to be penalized.

(b) You open 2♠. This is normal bidding in third seat. If you pass and give your LHO an easy ride, you may fall behind the other players holding your cards.

(c) Open 3♢. You would not do so in the first or second seat, but it makes good sense in third seat. If your LHO overcalls 3♠, his partner will have to guess whether he holds a 12-count or an 18-count.

(d) Should you open 3♣? Not on that suit! Many players would open 1♡, even with only four hearts. You expect to lose the auction and want a heart lead.

3.(a) Vulnerable, particularly in the first two seats, you need a fairly sound hand for a preempt. On this collection, with a poor suit, you should pass.

(b) This hand is worth 1♠. Partner will not expect this sort of playing strength for a weak two-bid in any seat.

(c) On this hand you need to preempt; on hand (b) you did not need to. So, open 3♣.

(d) Open 1♠. It is not suitable for 2♠ when you hold such good hearts. It is worth a full opening one-bid anyway.

5

CONTESTING THE PARTSCORE

Imagine that you were new to bridge and had so far played only a few friendly games in a home environment. A guy at work says that you can watch top-class bridge tournaments on the Internet. You have an hour to spare that evening and visit a site such as Bridge Base Online. You are in for a big surprise. On the majority of partscore deals, the players will fight like tigers!

Suppose the opponents stop bidding in 2♡. Even if you will go one down in a contract such as 2♠ or 3♣, it may well be worth bidding it. At matchpoints, losing 50 or 100 for one down undoubled will be better than conceding 110 to the opponents' successful heart contract. Also, you may push them to 3♡, perhaps giving you a chance of a plus score.

In this chapter, we will see when and how you should compete for a partscore contract.

Think before passing out a low-level contract

The opponents bid 1♡–2♡ and the opener then passes. What should your reaction be? The opponents have made no attempt to reach game, despite finding a fit. They are unlikely to hold more than 23 points between them; they may hold as few as 17-18 points. Your side holds close to half the high cards in the deck and it may be worthwhile to compete.

Another important incentive to compete is that the opponents have found an eight-card fit (at least). This means that the odds are excellent that you and your partner hold at least an eight-card fit. Look at it this way. You and your partner hold at most five hearts between you. That leaves at least twenty-one cards in the other three suits. Unless these are divided 7-7-7, you will hold an eight-card fit. Suppose you are West holding one of these hands:

(a) ♠ J 9 8 6 2 (b) ♠ A 10 4 2 (c) ♠ K Q 10 9 (d) ♠ 8 2
 ♡ 10 7 3   ♡ 9 2   ♡ 9 8 6   ♡ 9
 ◇ A 2   ◇ K J 8 2   ◇ Q J 6   ◇ K J 9 8 4
 ♣ K 9 3   ♣ Q 9 6   ♣ K 5 2   ♣ A 10 9 5 2

West	North	East	South
			1♡
pass	2♡	pass	pass
?			

On hand (a) you should bid 2♠. This is known as a 'balancing bid' because you are in the passout seat. Do not worry that you hold only 8 points. You know from the opponents' failure to look for game that your partner is likely to hold at least 10 points or so. He has at most two hearts and may well hold some spade support. Do not let the opponents buy the contract cheaply when they have found a fit!

On hand (b) you should double for takeout. On (c) you would prefer to compete with 2♠. Partner will be short in hearts and 2♠, even on a 4-3 fit, will play well. Since you did not overcall 1♠ on the first round, partner is entitled to remove to one of the minors when he is short in spades. If you double instead, you will end in the wrong contract when partner's shape is 3=2=4=4.

On hand (d) you bid 2NT, the Unusual Notrump to show length in both minor suits.

Non-vulnerable, you would compete on each of these hands at both IMPs and matchpoints. Vulnerable, playing matchpoints, most good players would bid just the same. Yes, there is some chance of being caught for a big number, but it is vital to contest partscores. On the odd occasion when you enter some unwelcome number in your minus column, it will only cost you one bad pairs score.

The time when you do need to exercise some restraint is when you are vulnerable at IMPs. The odds would still be in your favor if you bid 2♠ on (a) or double on (b). Some players would think it too much to compete on (c) or (d), though.

> **THINK ABOUT...**
>
> *The best time to compete for the partscore is when neither side is vulnerable. When partner is fairly weak, you will go down in 50s and the opponents could probably have made their contract. When partner is fairly strong, you will make your contract and the opponents would have gone down in 50s.*

Let's see a typical deal, where you hold hand (a) in the West seat:

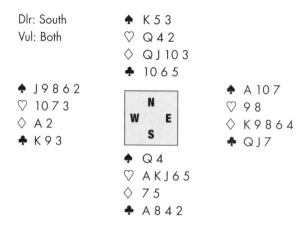

Dlr: South	♠ K 5 3
Vul: Both	♡ Q 4 2
	◇ Q J 10 3
	♣ 10 6 5

♠ J 9 8 6 2   ♠ A 10 7
♡ 10 7 3   ♡ 9 8
◇ A 2   ◇ K 9 8 6 4
♣ K 9 3   ♣ Q J 7

     ♠ Q 4
     ♡ A K J 6 5
     ◇ 7 5
     ♣ A 8 4 2

West	North	East	South
			1♡
pass	2♡	pass	pass
2♠	all pass		

The opponents stop at the two-level with a major-suit fit. You compete with 2♠, fully expecting your partner to hold close to a 10-count. He will hold at most two hearts, too, so there is a good chance to find him with spade support.

You can make 2♠, however they defend. If, instead, South decides to take the push to 3♡, he should go down — losing one spade, two diamonds and two clubs. By contesting the auction, you change a minus score into a plus score.

If the board arose in a matchpoint pairs, this might be the scoresheet:

N-S	E-W	Contract	By	Tricks	N-S score	E-W score	N-S MPs	E-W MPs
1	5	2♡	S	8	110		5.5	1.5
2	4	2♠	W	8		110	1	6
3	7	2♡	S	8	110		5.5	1.5
4	1	3♡	S	8		100	3	4
5	6	2♠	W	8		110	1	6
6	3	3♡	S	9	140		7	0
7	8	3♠	W	8	100		4	3
8	2	2♠	W	8		110	1	6

The two lucky N-S pairs who were allowed to play in the comfortable spot of 2♡ score 5.5 MPs. Three E-W pairs contested to 2♠ and played there, scoring eight tricks for the great score of 6 MPs. Two N-S pairs were pushed to 3♡ over 2♠, one going down and one allowed to make nine tricks on a misdefense. Finally, one E-W pair made the unsuccessful decision to persist to 3♠, having pushed N-S to a 3♡ contract that should have failed.

There, in one deal, you have the essence of competitive partscore bidding.

Balancing in fourth seat

Suppose your left-hand opponent opens 1♡ and this is the start to the auction:

West	North	East	South
1♡	pass	pass	?

West will probably do well if left to play in 1♡. He has at least five trumps and you will need to make seven tricks yourselves, even to get him one down. What is more, you know that you will be running into a bad trump break!

The high-card points are likely to be fairly evenly shared between your side and the opponents. East did not have enough points to respond and there is no reason to think that West has a particularly powerful hand. Remember that your partner may have been forced to pass on a balanced hand of up to 14 points, since a 1NT overcall shows 15 points or more. You should stretch to find a bid, even if your own hand is not particularly strong. You are entitled to hope that partner has a fair number of points and you can reach a playable contract.

The general idea is that the player in the fourth (balancing) seat should be willing to bid on about a king less than he would require in the second seat. Your partner (North) will allow for this when he makes his response, if any.

Suppose you hold one of these South hands:

(a) ♠ K 9 8 6 2
♡ 10 7 3
♢ 9 2
♣ A 8 7

(b) ♠ A 4
♡ K 10 4
♢ Q J 9 2
♣ Q 8 7 3

(c) ♠ Q 9 7 3
♡ 9 8
♢ A 10 8 2
♣ K J 6

West	North	East	South
1♡	pass	pass	?

On (a) you should balance with 1♠. You have only 7 points, yes, but if you 'borrow a king' from partner, that makes it 10 points — easily worth a one-level overcall.

On (b) you bid 1NT. Although such an overcall would require around 15-18 points in the second seat, you can again borrow a king and bid 1NT on 12-15 points.

Similarly, hand (c) is worth a balancing double. You have 10 points. Add another 3 and you have the 13 points that would justify a second-seat double on this hand shape. Let's see a typical full deal involving this hand:

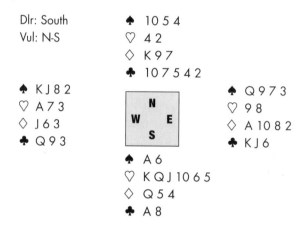

Dlr: South	♠ 10 5 4		
Vul: N-S	♡ 4 2		
	◇ K 9 7		
	♣ 10 7 5 4 2		

West hand: ♠ K J 8 2 ♡ A 7 3 ◇ J 6 3 ♣ Q 9 3

East hand: ♠ Q 9 7 3 ♡ 9 8 ◇ A 10 8 2 ♣ K J 6

South hand: ♠ A 6 ♡ K Q J 10 6 5 ◇ Q 5 4 ♣ A 8

West	North	East	South
			1♡
pass	pass	dbl	2♡
2♠	all pass		

It is no surprise that South has a strong hand. If he held much less, West would probably have been able to bid something on the first round. If you fail to balance on the East cards, South will pick up an easy +110 for eight tricks in 1♡. This will be an awful board for you, particularly at pairs. Your side has half the points in the pack and it is absolutely essential that you compete for the partscore. You are in the balancing seat, with 1♡ about to be passed out, so the responsibility is yours. You make a balancing takeout double.

South has a strong hand and is fully entitled to bid 2♡ (a contract that would in fact be made). West must now show some restraint on his hand. He holds 11 points, yes, but he has nine losers in his hand. Also, your double was made in the balancing seat and may be quite light. Correctly, he bids only 2♠ and this contract is passed out and just made, giving E-W a score of +110 instead of the −110 they would have collected if East had timidly passed.

Suppose the deal arose at matchpoints. This might be the scoresheet:

N-S	E-W	Contract	By	Tricks	N-S score	E-W score	N-S MPs	E-W MPs
1	5	1♡	S	8	110		6.5	0.5
2	4	2♠	W	8		110	2	5
3	7	3♡	S	8		100	4	3
4	1	2♠	W	8		110	2	5
5	6	3♠	W	8	100		5	2
6	3	1♡	S	8	110		6.5	0.5
7	8	3♡X	S	8		200	0	7
8	2	2♠	W	8		110	2	5

Two South players were allowed to play in 1♡. They picked up a shared top of 6.5 MPs, giving those Easts who failed to balance a (well deserved!) shared bottom of 0.5 MPs.

Three E-W pairs competed to 2♠ and played there, making +110 for 5 MPs. Two South players took the push to 3♡, going one down. Undoubled, this scored −100, which was better than −110 for N-S making 2♠.

N-S Pair 7 were out of luck when West made a bold penalty double of 3♡. The resultant +200 was a top score for E-W Pair 8, giving them a full 7 MPs. We will see in Chapter 10 that a score of 200 usually gives you a magnificent matchpoint score on a partscore deal. Known as the 'Magic 200', it encourages players to make somewhat risky penalty doubles of vulnerable opponents.

Finally, E-W Pair 6 went too high in 3♠ (perhaps over 3♡ by South... we will never know the full auction!) They scored only 2 MPs.

The Law of Total Trumps

When neither side has game values, a valuable guideline helps you to judge how strongly to compete. You should bid to the level dictated by your **combined trump length**. Suppose your side holds five spades opposite four. That's a total of nine trumps, so you should generally compete to the nine-trick (3♠) level even when you hold only half the points in the deck.

Let's see a typical competitive deal that illustrates this:

```
Dlr: West          ♠ 10
Vul: Both          ♡ K Q 4 2
                   ◇ 9 8 5 2
                   ♣ 10 7 4 2

♠ K Q 7 2                          ♠ A 9 8 5 4
♡ A 9 7          ┌─────────┐       ♡ 10 6 5
◇ A 10 7 3       │    N    │       ◇ Q J 6
♣ J 6           │ W     E │       ♣ 8 5
                 │    S    │
                 └─────────┘
                   ♠ J 6 3
                   ♡ J 8 3
                   ◇ K 4
                   ♣ A K Q 9 3
```

West	North	East	South
1◇	pass	1♠	2♣
2♠	3♣	3♠	all pass

N-S hold nine clubs between them. As you see, they are correct to compete to the nine-trick level because they can make 3♣ even on best defense (East overtakes the ♠K lead with the ♠A and switches to the ◇Q. The defenders then claim their two diamond tricks before declarer can set up a discard on the hearts.)

THINK ABOUT...

The 'support double' allows your partner to know whether you hold three-card or four-card support for his major suit. After a start of 1♣ (pass) 1♠ (2◇), for example, the opener will double on any hand with three-card spade support and raise the spades directly with four-card support. After a double, the opener can indicate his overall strength on the next round.

East can place West with four-card spade support, because his partnership plays Support Doubles. In other words, a double by West would show any hand with three-card spade support; all direct spade raises promise four trumps. Despite holding only 7 HCPs, East knows that his side holds a total of nine spades. He too is therefore willing to advance to the nine-trick level (3♠). Nine tricks are made in this contract when the diamond finesse wins — no more than nine because declarer can score only three diamond tricks.

You may think it strange that the number of trumps plays such a large part in these competitive bidding decisions, rather than the number of points. That's because any extra points will serve equally well in defense.

Similarly, the favorable position of the cards (or otherwise) does not tend to affect matters unduly. Suppose North had held the ◇K on the above hand. A contract of 3♠ would then go down (provided the defenders knocked out the ♡A before the diamonds were established). But N-S would then have been able to make 4♣ on their cards.

When you know that your side has at least a nine-card fit, it is often a good idea to bid to the limit immediately. By doing so, you take bidding space away from the opponents.

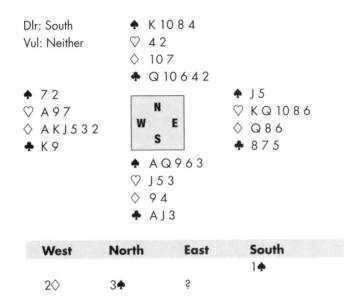

West	North	East	South
			1♠
2◇	3♠	?	

E-W can make game in hearts but it is not so easy for them after your space-consuming raise to 3♠ on the North cards. Some Easts would pass now, some might bid 4◇, and others hope that a competitive double would work well. Suppose instead that you bid only 2♠ on the North cards. The opponents would have an extra level of bidding available to evaluate their prospects. In particular, East would have the option of bidding 3♡.

Remember that North's 3♠ does not show a good hand. With a sound raise to that level, he would bid 3◇, instead. (Some players use 2NT to show a sound raise with four-card support, 3◇ to show a sound raise with three-card support.)

THINK ABOUT...

The least favorable time to compete for the partscore is when both sides are vulnerable. When partner is fairly weak, you will go down in 100s. Losing 200 will be more than the value of the opponents' contract. When partner is fairly strong, you may make your contract but the opponents might well have gone down in 100s, possibly losing 200.

- When the points are equally divided between the sides, or nearly so, be prepared to compete to the level indicated by your combined trump holding. If you and your partner hold nine spades between you, compete to the nine-trick level (bidding 3♠).

- To enable your side to judge how high to compete, it is important to know whether partner has three-card or four-card support. One useful convention in this area is the Support Double. After an overcall by the fourth player, the opener indicates three-card support for responder's major by doubling.

- You should always be reluctant to let the opponents play in a trump fit at the two-level. The responsibility for contesting the auction often lies with the player in the passout (balancing) seat. He can compete with an overcall or a takeout double on fewer values than in other circumstances. It is reasonable to assume that partner holds some useful cards when the opponents sell out at the two-level.

Test Yourself

Assume you are playing matchpoints on these five problems:

1. WEST

♠ J 6
♡ K 5
◇ K 10 8 7 6 2
♣ K 9 4

West	North	East	South
	1♠	pass	pass
?			

Both sides are vulnerable. What action, if any, will you take?

2. WEST

♠ K Q 7 5 4
♡ K J 7 5 4
◇ —
♣ Q 10 9

West	North	East	South
			1♡
1♠	1NT	2♠	pass
pass	3◇	pass	pass
?			

The deal comes from a European Open Mixed Pairs final. Neither side is vulnerable. What action will you take on these West cards now?

3. WEST

♠ Q J 6
♡ 10 7 4
◇ A Q 5
♣ J 9 8 3

West	North	East	South
		1♠	2♡
2♠	3♡	pass	pass
?			

Neither side is vulnerable. What action will you take on these West cards now?

4. WEST

♠ K J 7 6
♡ 10 7
◇ A Q 5
♣ 10 9 8 3

West	North	East	South
	1♣	pass	1♡
pass	2♡	pass	pass
?			

N-S are vulnerable. Would you take any action on the West cards now?

5. WEST

♠ J 9 8 7 4
♡ A 5 2
◇ A
♣ K Q 8 4

West	North	East	South
			pass
1♠	pass	2♠	2NT
?			

Neither side is vulnerable. Would you take any action on the West cards now?

ANSWERS

1. You would not make a vulnerable overcall in the second seat on these values, with a broken diamond suit. In the balancing seat you are worth 2◊, whether you are playing IMPs or matchpoints. You simply cannot afford to let North play in 1♠, often making an easy plus score. Your side holds around half the points and you have a six-card suit.

2. The player sitting West competed with 3♠ on these cards. Was that right, do you think? He held a five-loser hand, it's true, but several factors suggested that he should pass. Firstly, he held only five trumps — the normal minimum for his one-level overcall. Secondly, the opponent on his left had bid 1NT suggesting at least one spade stopper. Thirdly, his side suit of hearts had been bid by the opponents and would not break helpfully. Finally, his diamond void suggested that the 3◊ contract might go down. His partner actually held

    ♠ 8 6 3   ♡ 3   ◊ K Q 7 6 4   ♣ J 8 7 3

    North's 3◊ could have been made with good play, but 3♠ was doubled and went 300 down for a near-bottom score.

3. You have 10 points and partner has opened the bidding. That is not enough to justify advancing to 3♠ now, because you expect to hold only eight trumps between the hands. (If partner held six spades, he would probably have bid 3♠ himself.) Your extra high-card values will fare just as well in defense. From what you can judge, the most likely result is that both 3♡ and 3♠ will go one down. It is impossible to judge such matters accurately, and only a player who likes life in the fast lane would venture a double of 3♡. It is important to aim for a plus score on such deals. Increasing your score from +50 to +100, by doubling, would not make much difference.

4. The opponents have found a heart fit and stopped at the two-level. They are unlikely to hold 23 points between them and may hold something like 12 opposite 6. Since you can place your partner with several points, you are entitled to compete with a takeout double now. You expect partner to respond either 2♠ or 3◊ now. If

he held only three spades and four diamonds, he might well choose 2♠, to keep the bidding one level lower.

5.   In the 2013 Polish Grand Prix Pairs, West contested with 3♠. His partner held about what could be expected:

♠ K Q 5 ♡ 9 7 6 ◇ 10 8 7 4 3 ♣ J 7

The player on his left held all five missing spades, doubled the contract and scored very well for +300. Why was it wrong for West to bid 3♠? Firstly, he held no extra length in trumps and could expect the total trumps to be eight; if East happened to hold four-card spade support, he could bid 3♠ on his hand. Secondly, West held defensive values that would be useful against a minor-suit contract. Thirdly, the Unusual Notrump overcall had warned him of the bad breaks that he would face. Both 3♣ and 3◇ would have gone down.

6

CHOOSING THE RIGHT GAME

When is it right to prefer a major-suit game to 3NT? Does your choice vary between matchpoint and IMP games? When should you bid a minor-suit game instead of 3NT? These are the questions we will consider in this chapter.

Should I bid 3NT or four of a major with a 4-4 fit?

Let's suppose that you have a 4-4 fit in one of the major suits — spades, for example. You will often score at least one trick more by playing in 4♠ rather than 3NT. Why is that? Suppose the trump suit is solid. It will bring you four tricks if you play in 3NT. In 4♠, you may be able to take a ruff in one hand; this will give you five spade tricks rather than four. Look at this typical deal:

```
Dlr: South        ♠ K J 8 3        Matchpoints
Vul: Both         ♡ K 4
                  ◇ A 6 2
                  ♣ 9 4 3 2

♠ 7 6 4                              ♠ 10 5
♡ J 9 6 2            N               ♡ Q 8 7 5
◇ Q J 10 7      W         E          ◇ 9 8 5 3
♣ J 8               S               ♣ K Q 5

                  ♠ A Q 9 2
                  ♡ A 10 3
                  ◇ K 4
                  ♣ A 10 7 6
```

West	North	East	South
			1NT
pass	2♣	pass	2♠
pass	4♠	all pass	

Playing in 3NT, a red-suit lead would hold you to the nine top tricks that you were dealt. You could not set up an extra club trick before the defenders scored two diamonds (or hearts) and two clubs. You would score +600.

Playing in 4♠, you enjoy two advantages. The first is that you will score five spade tricks, including a heart ruff in the North hand. The second is that you *will* now have time to set up a second club trick. Your trumps will protect you in both hearts and diamonds. When a third round is led, you will able to ruff in one hand or the other. So, on this particular layout, you would actually score two more tricks by playing in spades. You would pick up +650 for eleven tricks made.

When both hands have 4-3-3-3 shape, you will usually fare better in 3NT. That's because you will not be able to score a ruff to give you five trump tricks instead of four. Here is a typical deal:

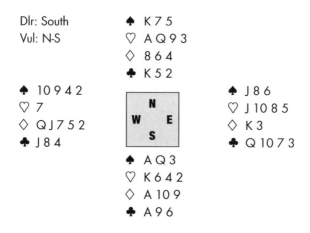

Dlr: South	♠ K 7 5
Vul: N-S	♡ A Q 9 3
	◇ 8 6 4
	♣ K 5 2

♠ 10 9 4 2   ♠ J 8 6
♡ 7   ♡ J 10 8 5
◇ Q J 7 5 2   ◇ K 3
♣ J 8 4   ♣ Q 10 7 3

♠ A Q 3
♡ K 6 4 2
◇ A 10 9
♣ A 9 6

West	**North**	**East**	**South**
			1NT
pass	2♣	pass	2♡
pass	4♡	all pass	

In 3NT you would start with nine tricks and that is all you can make, scoring +600. How would you fare in 4♡? You cannot score a ruff in either hand and will score exactly the same nine tricks. That will be –100 in the major-suit game.

At matchpoints, it would make no difference if the hearts were 3-2. You would make 4♡ in that case, yes, but that would be only +620. In 3NT you would also make a trick more and +630 would beat the pairs in the 4-4 heart fit.

What do we conclude from that? Most experts do not bid Stayman when their shape is 4-3-3-3. How does that grab you? It would work well on the deal we have just seen, because the hand opposite also happened to be 4-3-3-3. If instead the opener's hand was 4-4-3-2, which is more likely, you might well score a ruff in his doubleton suit and overtake the declarers in 3NT.

There are two hidden advantages in raising to 3NT on such hands. Firstly, bidding Stayman may give useful information to the opponents when you do not find a fit. Secondly, defenders are more likely to give a trick away when on lead against 3NT. Let's take a closer look at this 'Stayman or not' dilemma.

Should I bid Stayman with 4-3-3-3 shape?

Partner opens a 15-17 point 1NT and you hold this hand as responder:

♠K95 ♡Q1085 ◇A94 ♣J43

Should you raise to 3NT or seek a 4-4 heart fit by bidding Stayman?

Ask different players and you will get different answers. A computer simulation of 5000 deals where the opener does hold four hearts, giving you a 4-4 fit, will tell us whether you will fare better in 3NT or 4♡:

Playing in a 4-4 heart fit, with this North hand

Contract	Makes	Avg tricks	MPs	IMPs (V)	IMPs (NV)
3NT	66.1%	9.0	51.8%	+1.2	+0.9
4♡	55.5%	9.6	48.2%	−1.2	−0.9

As you see, 3NT is a hugely better contract at IMPs. It will succeed 66.1% of the time, compared with only 55.5% for 4♡. When you play in hearts, you do make an extra 0.6 tricks on average. This does not make the heart game a better contract at matchpoints because when you score nine tricks in 4♡ and eight in 3NT, you will score the same for your 'one down'. 3NT is also slightly the better matchpoint contract, giving you an average 51.8% score compared with 48.2% for 4♡. We conclude that you should not bid Stayman on hands similar to the one shown above.

Much of the advantage for 3NT accrues when the opener also holds 3=4=3=3 shape. Suppose you play a sophisticated system where you can diagnose whether partner has this shape. (For example, you can play that 1NT–2♣–2♡–3♠ is either a slam try in hearts, or a 3=4=3=3 hand looking for the best game. The opener must bid 3NT when he is also 3=4=3=3. When the 4-4 fit is in spades instead, you bid 1NT–2♣–2♠–3♡.)

Let's see now whether 4♡ is better than 3NT when you are 3=4=3=3 but have discovered that partner is not. He will then hold a doubleton somewhere, which may allow you to score an extra ruffing trick or two.

Playing in a 4-4 heart fit, with this North hand (South not 3=4=3=3)

Contract	Makes	Avg tricks	MPs	IMPs (V)	IMPs (NV)
3NT	66.4%	9.0	47.1%	+0.2	+0.1
4♡	62.8%	9.8	52.9%	−0.2	−0.1

3NT is still the better contract (marginally) at IMPs. It will succeed more often, and the value of a game swing is significant at that form of scoring. At matchpoints, the 0.8 extra tricks per deal give a slight edge to 4♡; you will score 52.9% in the long run instead of 47.1%.

Was Terence Reese right?

Many experts decline to bid Stayman on 4-3-3-3 shape. Terence Reese went further. When watching top invitational events such as the *Sunday Times* Pairs, he would pour scorn on contestants who used Stayman on certain 4-4-3-2 hands. 'Did you see that?' he would exclaim, far too loudly because he was deaf in his later years. 'Absurd! The man bid Stayman.' Was this another of his famed eccentricities or was there some sense to it? Let's find out. Partner opens a 15-17 point 1NT and you hold this hand as responder:

♠K974 ♡KJ ♢Q1072 ♣J83

Should you raise to 3NT or use Stayman to seek a 4-4 spade fit? The fact that the heart doubleton contains two honors reduces the chance that a heart ruff will provide an extra trick. The presence of minor honors and the lack of an ace also tilt the odds towards notrump. These are the results from a simulation that evaluates 5000 deals where Stayman would locate a 4-4 spade fit:

3NT or 4♠, in a 4-4 spade fit with this responding hand?

Contract	Makes	Avg tricks	MPs	IMPs (V)	IMPs (NV)
3NT	61.2%	8.8	48.9%	+0.3	+0.2
4♠	55.5%	9.6	51.1%	−0.3	−0.2

Ah, not so eccentric, then! 3NT is more likely to make and is the better contract at IMPs. 4♠ has a small advantage at matchpoints. The most common result, occurring on 21% of the deals, is a swing of +20 for 420 against 400, or 450 against 430 (or the matching scores when vulnerable). Now look at this responding hand:

$\spadesuit$ Q 6 5 $\heartsuit$ 10 8 6 3 $\diamondsuit$ A Q $\clubsuit$ K 8 7 3

You have a strong doubleton, your major is weak and there may be too many trump losers in 4$\heartsuit$. Should you make a Stayman response? Let's see.

Playing in a 4-4 heart fit, with this responding hand

Contract	Makes	Avg tricks	MPs	IMPs (V)	IMPs (NV)
3NT	76.4%	9.3	46.5%	+0.4	+0.3
4$\heartsuit$	70.6%	10.0	53.5%	−0.4	−0.3

As on the previous hand, 3NT is more likely to make and is better at IMPs. Playing pairs, you should still choose the suit game. On 33% of deals 4$\heartsuit$ will give you the matchpoints with a +20 advantage (620 against 600, for example). On 23% of the deals 3NT will give you a +10 advantage (630 against 620).

Should I bid 3NT or four of a major with a 5-3 fit?

Which game should you choose with a 5-3 major-suit fit? The first trick at notrump gives you a precious extra 10 points. Against that, the major-suit game can offer two advantages previously noted: you may be able to take a ruff in the short hand; you may be able to use your trumps to stop the defenders from cashing side-suit tricks. One deal proves nothing, it's true, but look at this deal:

Dlr: South
Vul: Neither

Matchpoints

```
                    ♠ 8 3
                    ♥ A J 10 3 2
                    ◇ J 8 7
                    ♣ A 8 5
  ♠ Q J 5 2                        ♠ K 9 7 6
  ♥ 9 5            N               ♥ 8 7 4
  ◇ 9 5 2      W       E           ◇ A 6 4
  ♣ Q 9 6 2        S               ♣ K 10 7
                    ♠ A 10 4
                    ♥ K Q 6
                    ◇ K Q 10 3
                    ♣ J 4 3
```

West	North	East	South
			1NT
pass	2$\diamondsuit$	pass	2$\heartsuit$
pass	3NT	all pass	

With no ruffing value in his hand, our first declarer decides to leave 3NT, despite holding three-card heart support. West leads the ♠2 and declarer can count seven top tricks. He wins the ♠K with the ♠A, reading West for a four-card suit after his lead of the ♠2, and clears the diamond suit. The defenders win and score three spades, holding declarer to a score of +400.

Suppose that at another table, South chooses to bid 4♡ instead of passing 3NT. Whichever black suit West chooses to lead, declarer will be able to draw trumps and set up the diamonds, discarding a black loser from the North hand. He will score five hearts, three diamonds and two black aces for +420, beating the guy in 3NT. Why did he do better? Because dummy's trumps protected him against losing three spade tricks.

Well, you can move cards around to get a deal where you score more matchpoints in 3NT. One deal proves nothing, as we know. The only way to tell whether South should pass 3NT or correct to 4♡ on the hand above is to run a computer simulation.

Playing in a 5-3 heart fit, with this South hand

Contract	Makes	Avg tricks	MPs	IMPs (V)	IMPs (NV)
3NT	70.4%	9.3	55.4%	–0.44	–0.40
4♡	72.0%	10.0	44.6%	+0.44	+0.40

These numbers may seem confusing at first glance. **3NT is much better than 4♡ at matchpoints**, scoring 55.4% to 44.6%. This is despite the fact that 4♡ makes more tricks on average (10.0 to 9.3) and is successful slightly more often (72.0% to 70.5%). How can that be?

The explanation is that when both contracts make ten tricks, 3NT takes all the matchpoints for its +630 against +620 (or +430 against +420). A difference of only 10 aggregate points is not worth 1 IMP, so **at IMPs 4♡ fares better than 3NT.**

Should I bid 3NT or five of a minor?

Even when you are playing IMPs and looking only for the game that is most likely to make, there is good reason to veer towards 3NT rather than five of a minor. The reason is clear — you have to make only nine tricks rather than eleven. Let's look at a deal to fix this idea in our minds:

```
Dlr: South        ♠ 10 4 2
Vul: Neither      ♡ K J 7 3
                  ◇ A 10 8 6
                  ♣ Q 8
♠ Q J 5 3                        ♠ K 9 7 6
♡ 9 5 2          ┌─────────┐     ♡ Q 10 8 4
◇ 9 5            │    N    │     ◇ 2
♣ A 9 6 2        │  W   E  │     ♣ K 10 7 5
                 │    S    │
                 └─────────┘
                  ♠ A 8
                  ♡ A 6
                  ◇ K Q J 7 4 3
                  ♣ J 4 3
```

West	North	East	South
			1◇
pass	1♡	pass	3◇
pass	4◇	pass	4♡
pass	5◇	all pass	

It may seem natural for North to raise the diamonds, but he has a balanced hand and is facing only about 16 points or so in partner's hand. Even though he has no real stopper in either black suit, 3NT is the percentage action in any form of the game.

As you see, 3NT is an easy make; there are nine tricks on top. If you reach 5◇ instead, you can score a tenth trick by ruffing a club, but you will need to finesse the ♡J successfully to dispose of your spade loser. Even if the ♡Q is onside, you will still score only +400. If the game is matchpoints and North plays in 3NT at other tables, East will sometimes lead a club and that may result in an overtrick for +430.

Does anything else occur to you about the auction shown above, particularly if the event is a matchpoint pairs? There is a good case for South opening 1NT instead of 1◇. That would allow the easy auction 1NT–2♣–2◇–3NT, reaching the top spot.

The fact that making ten tricks in 3NT will allow declarer to outscore rivals who score as many as twelve tricks in five of a minor, means that you can afford to take a slight risk when you head for the notrump game.

Suppose your partner opens a 15-17 point 1NT and you hold this hand:

♠9 ♡Q 5 ◇K 10 9 8 6 5 3 ♣A 9 3

You want to be in game, at least. If you had to judge the best contract immediately, would you favor 3NT, 5◇, or possibly 6◇?

First, let's compare the two game contracts, again using a 5000-deal simulation:

3NT or 5◊, with seven-card diamonds opposite 1NT

Contract	Makes	Avg tricks	MPs	IMPs (V)	IMPs (NV)
3NT	70.8%	9.8	71.4%	–0.2	+0.1
5◊	78.6%	11.2	28.6%	+0.2	–0.1

Just look at the percentages when playing matchpoints! If the whole field were divided between 3NT and 5◊, those in the notrump game would score 71.4% on average. Those stranded in 5◊ would pick up only 28.6%.

At IMPs the situation is much closer, because the 5◊ bidders will pick up game swings when their game makes and 3NT fails. 5◊ is a better prospect when vulnerable, by 0.2 IMPs per board. 3NT is marginally ahead when non-vulnerable, because the 1-IMP and 2-IMP swings add up to more than the smaller number of non-vulnerable game swings. (The three most common results are +460 v +400, +490 v +420 and +430 v +400.)

One further question arises. Since you will score only a miserable 28.6% for stopping in 5◊ at matchpoints, should you advance to 6◊ once you have reached 5◊ (looking for a slam) and realize that those in 3NT will do better?

Bidding 6◊ when you have left 3NT behind

Contract	Makes	Avg tricks	MPs	IMPs (V)	IMPs (NV)
3NT	70.8%	9.8	54.4%	+1.4	+1.6
6◊	31.4%	11.2	45.6%	–1.4	–1.6

That's interesting. Even though 6◊ will succeed only 31.4% of the time (compared with 78.6% for 5◊), you should choose the small slam at matchpoints once you have left 3NT behind! You will score a top when the slam makes and pick up an average of 45.6% of the matchpoints, compared with 28.6% if you stop in 5◊. (At IMPs you should stay in 5◊.)

Remember that these are figures only for the particular North hand shown on the previous page. Alter the hand and the figures will move up or down a bit. However, the general principle of bidding in this area is clear: prefer 3NT to 5◊ even if this may seem a bit risky. Once you have strayed past 3NT and reached 5◊ at matchpoints, consider attempting a rescue act by bidding 6◊.

When is it right to play in a minor-suit game, then? One occasion arises when your own bidding makes it clear that no stopper is held in one of the side suits. On the next deal, the vehicle is a splinter bid:

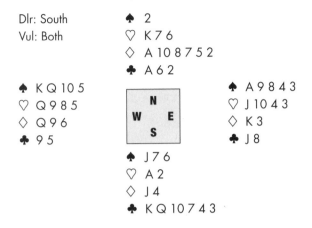

Dlr: South
Vul: Both

North
♠ 2
♡ K 7 6
♢ A 10 8 7 5 2
♣ A 6 2

West
♠ K Q 10 5
♡ Q 9 8 5
♢ Q 9 6
♣ 9 5

East
♠ A 9 8 4 3
♡ J 10 4 3
♢ K 3
♣ J 8

South
♠ J 7 6
♡ A 2
♢ J 4
♣ K Q 10 7 4 3

West	North	East	South
			1♣
pass	1♢	pass	2♣
pass	3♠	pass	5♣
all pass			

South's 2♣ rebid implies six clubs, since he cannot bid a major or raise the diamonds and he has not opened or rebid 1NT. North's 3♠ splinter bid agrees clubs as trumps and shows at most one card in spades. Two things are now clear to South. The first is that his side does not hold a spade stopper. The second is that he may be able to score two extra tricks by ruffing spade losers in the dummy.

Giving no thought whatsoever to 3NT after this start, he leaps to the club game. Even if West leads a trump and continues with another trump when he wins the first round of spades, the game will be made by setting up the diamond suit.

- With game values and 4-3-3-3 shape including a four-card major, you should raise directly to 3NT rather than bid Stayman.

- With game values and 4-4-3-2 including one or more four-card majors, lean towards 3NT at IMPs when your doubleton is strong and your trumps are weak. Look for a 4-4 fit at matchpoints.

- When partner uses a transfer sequence to offer a choice of 3NT or a major-suit game, prefer 3NT at matchpoints when you have three-card support and 4-3-3-3 shape. Bid the major-suit game at IMPs.

- Even when you hold a seven-card minor suit, facing 1NT, it is rarely right to prefer game in that suit to 3NT at matchpoints. At IMPs, there is little in it and you should seek the safer game.

- If you find yourself in 5♣ or 5◇ at matchpoints, when you fear that much of the field will be scoring more in 3NT, consider bidding a small slam in your suit even when this contract will be against the odds.

Teſt Yourſelf

1. What will you bid next on these three West hands at matchpoints?

West	North	East	South
1NT	pass	2◇	pass
2♡	pass	3NT	pass
?			

(a) ♠ Q 10 3
♡ K J 4
◇ A Q 10 2
♣ K 8 7

(b) ♠ A K 7 2
♡ J 8 6
◇ A 5
♣ Q J 7 2

(c) ♠ K 3
♡ A 9 2
◇ Q 10 6 4
♣ A K J 2

2. You partner opens 1NT. What is your matchpoint bidding plan on these three hands?

(a) ♠ A 9 4
♡ 10 8 6 2
◇ Q J 4
♣ K 7 2

(b) ♠ 10 3
♡ K Q 10 7 3
◇ K 4
♣ Q 10 7 2

(c) ♠ A Q
♡ J 7 4 2
◇ K Q 8 3
♣ Q 5 3

3. What will you bid next on this West hand at matchpoints?

WEST	West	East
♠ 6	1♡	1NT
♡ A K 8 7 2	2♣	2◇
◇ A 10 2	?	
♣ A K 10 5		

4. What will you bid next on this West hand at matchpoints?

WEST	West	East
♠ K 7 2		1◇
♡ A K 10 5	1♡	2◇
◇ Q 9 6	?	
♣ 10 8 7		

ANSWERS

1.(a) You have good reason to expect 3NT to be better than 4♡. Your 4-3-3-3 shape means that you will have no ruffing value to create an extra trick. You should pass.

(b) Now 4♡ looks better. Your hearts are weak and you may have to concede one or more heart tricks to set up that suit at notrump. You have a ruffing value in diamonds that may create an extra trick, playing in hearts.

(c) Your hand is excellent for hearts! It is not generally a good idea to break the transfer when you hold only three-card trump support. Now, though, you are entitled to show that you have an excellent maximum for hearts, along with a ruffing value, just in case partner can then show slam interest. You should cuebid 4♣.

2.(a) You should raise to 3NT. Your hearts are weak; if you find a 4-4 fit and play in 4♡, you might go down due to too many trump losers and find that 3NT was laydown. You have no ruffing value. You have good stoppers in all the other three suits. No contest!

(b) You begin with 2◊, seeking a heart fit. What should you say when partner rebids 2♡? You should bid 3NT, not 3♣. Only introduce a minor suit when your hand suggests that playing in that suit may be an option. At matchpoints, this means that you can foresee a possible minor-suit slam. With 2=5=2=4 shape, also on some minimum 3=5=1=4 game raises, the choice is between 4♡ and 3NT. Show this by rebidding 3NT.

(c) You should respond 3NT at matchpoints, even though you hold a four-card major and your shape is not 3=4=3=3. What are the indications that 3NT will be better? Your doubleton (♠AQ) is a strong one, so it may not give you a ruffing value in hearts. Your hearts are weak. Also, you have points to spare and this should ensure plenty of tricks in notrump.

3. Partner has signed off with long diamonds. You have a great fit for diamonds and must investigate the best game. Your most accurate continuation is a splinter bid of 3♠, showing the spade shortage. If partner then bids 3NT, you can pass. Otherwise, head for 5◊.

4. How good will 3NT be? A simulation shows that it will succeed 53% of the time (less than I had expected). If notrump is your only target, this suggests that you should bid only 2NT now. When partner accepts, 3NT will have prospects considerably higher than 53%. When your invitation is declined, 3NT will not be worth bidding.

How about 5◊? It is only a 35% chance and not worth chasing.

7

Dislodging Opponents from 1NT

It is a fact of matchpoint life that the declarer in 1NT will often score a good board. Suppose he goes one down, losing either 50 or 100 (depending on the vulnerability). There is then a good chance that the opponents could have scored 110 or 140, playing in their best trump fit. When you are non-vulnerable, you may score above average for going two down in 1NT, losing 100. It will often be difficult for the opponents to double you, particularly when their strength is divided.

This is not an idle observation. When an opponent opens 1NT, you should be unwilling to let him play there, possibly making a good score at your expense. You should strain to enter the bidding, even when this may incur some risk. Remember that it does not matter unduly if you suffer a horrendous −800 at matchpoints. It is just one bad board. If your slightly risky interventions over 1NT improve your score on three or four other boards, this will be ample compensation.

You probably already have a favorite convention for bidding over 1NT. By all means, stick with it! Otherwise, you may perhaps like to try the Cappelletti Defense to 1NT. Let's take a look at that.

The Cappelletti Defense

When an opponent has opened 1NT, either weak or strong, your side (in both the second and fourth seats) may intervene according to this method:

2♣	shows a single-suited hand (six cards are assumed in the suit)
2◇	shows both the majors (at least 5-4 or 4-5)
2♡	shows hearts and an unspecified minor (at least 5-4 or 4-5)
2♠	shows spades and an unspecified minor (at least 5-4 or 4-5)
2NT	shows both minor suits (at least 5-5)

Double for penalties

Since you expect to start with a double on most hands of 15+ points, the two-level overcalls tend to be based on weaker hands (around 9-14 points).

When you are non-vulnerable, you can risk entering the auction on quite weak hands. Remember that you expect to score poorly if your opponent is allowed to play in 1NT. Suppose that the bidding has started:

West	North	East	South
			1NT
?			

... and, sitting West, you hold one of these hands:

(1)	♠ K 5	(2)	♠ Q 10 8 7	(3)	♠ 9 4	(4)	♠ K 10 7 4 3
	♡ Q J 8 7 4 2		♡ 7 5		♡ 7		♡ A J 8 7 2
	◇ 10 8 4		◇ A 3		◇ A J 9 8 2		◇ 10 6
	♣ Q 5		♣ K 7 5 4 2		♣ K Q 7 6 2		♣ 8

None of these hands is particularly special, but you should happily bid on all of them. You show a single-suited hand with 2♣ on (1), spades and a minor with 2♠ on (2). With hand (3) you bid 2NT to show both minors (2NT). Hand (4) is ideal for 2◇, showing both majors.

'Wait a minute,' you say, 'surely the vulnerability makes a difference?'

It does, of course, but less so when you are playing matchpoints rather than IMPs. It is not so easy for the opponents to catch you with a penalty double. Even if they do occasionally take you for a big number, the cost will be just one bad board. So, be a bit more careful when you are vulnerable, but don't retreat into your shell unduly.

Let's see a typical matchpoint deal featuring the Cappelletti convention:

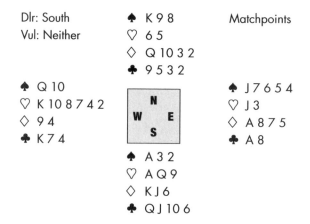

```
Dlr: South        ♠ K 9 8         Matchpoints
Vul: Neither      ♡ 6 5
                  ◇ Q 10 3 2
                  ♣ 9 5 3 2

♠ Q 10                            ♠ J 7 6 5 4
♡ K 10 8 7 4 2      N             ♡ J 3
◇ 9 4          W       E          ◇ A 8 7 5
♣ K 7 4            S              ♣ A 8

                  ♠ A 3 2
                  ♡ A Q 9
                  ◇ K J 6
                  ♣ Q J 10 6
```

West	North	East	South
			1NT
2♣	pass	2♢	pass
2♡	all pass		

West shows an unspecified single-suiter. East makes the standard response of 2♢, asking which suit partner holds, and West duly rebids 2♡. On this particular layout the contract cannot be beaten and E-W score +110. Suppose West had been less adventurous and South had played in 1NT. This would be an easy make on a heart lead, with declarer scoring two hearts, three diamonds and the ♠AK. The E-W pair would then score −90.

Of course, this is just one possible layout and proves nothing on its own. The point to note is that E-W have several ways of obtaining a good board in 2♡. They would score well if 2♡ went one down for −50 and 1NT was making at other tables. Making 2♡ would be a good result if 1NT was going one or two down at other tables. The odds are in your favor if you enter the auction with the West hand above.

How do you respond to the various Cappelletti bids? In general, you will seek a playable fit at the minimum level and not attempt to bid game (against a strong 1NT, at any rate) unless you have a good trump fit.

Your options opposite a one-suiter 2♣ are to ask for the suit with 2♢, or to show a respectable major suit of your own by responding 2♡ or 2♠. The overcaller must bear in mind when he bids 2♣ with a long club suit, that he will usually have to play in 3♣.

Suppose partner has overcalled 2♢, showing both majors:

West	North	East	South
	1NT	2♢	pass
?			

... and, sitting West at matchpoints, you hold one of these hands:

(1) ♠ K 5	(2) ♠ Q 10 8	(3) ♠ K 10 9 4 3	(4) ♠ 9 2
♡ 7 4	♡ 9 6	♡ A 8	♡ 7
♢ J 9 8 5 2	♢ A 9 8 3	♢ 3	♢ A Q 9 8 6 4
♣ Q 9 6 3	♣ K Q 5 4	♣ Q 9 8 6 4	♣ J 10 6 5

On hand (1) you should respond 2♡ rather than 2♠. Remember that partner may hold four spades and five hearts. When you are expecting a minus score and are worried that you may be doubled, keep the bidding low. If you are doubled in 2♡, you can then consider bidding 2♠.

On hand (2) respond just 2♠. Partner's expected range is 9-14, yes, but what is the chance that he will hold 14 points opposite your 11 when North has opened a strong 1NT? This table shows the likely point count for the East hand:

HCPs	9	10	11	12	13	14
Frequency	36.6%	28.0%	18.5%	10.7%	5.2%	1.0%

If partner bids on all 9-14 point hands with 5-4 or 4-5 shape in the majors (assumed in the above table), his average point count will be only 10.2 points. Even if your partner would pass on some hands with 9 and 10 points, the odds are hugely against him holding enough for game. Also, when you hold three spades and two hearts, partner will hold a five-card spade suit only 52% of the time (five-card hearts 63%).

On (3) you have a big spade fit and a splendid doubleton ace in partner's other suit. You are worth a leap to 4♠. On (4) you have no wish to play in a major suit. You should pass 2◊, allowing partner to play that contract with six trumps in the dummy!

When partner bids 2♡ or 2♠, showing that suit and an unspecified minor, your most common action will be to pass. Even if you have only two-card support, it may be best to stay at the two-level. When instead you are interested in playing in his minor side suit, you can bid 2NT to ask which suit this is.

Suppose the bidding starts:

West	North	East	South
	1NT	2♠	pass
?			

... and, sitting West, you hold one of these hands:

(1) ♠ A 5	(2) ♠ Q 8	(3) ♠ J 3	(4) ♠ J 9 2
♡ K 10 4	♡ A 9 7 2	♡ Q 10 7 5 3	♡ K 2
◊ J 9 8 5	◊ Q 10 5	◊ 10 3	◊ A J 6 2
♣ 10 7 6 3	♣ J 8 7 3	♣ K Q 9 4	♣ J 10 6 5

With hand (1) you are assured of an eight-card (or longer) fit in one of the minors. Should you bid 2NT to ask for partner's minor, or pass 2♠? Your partner will hold five spades 66% of the time, but even then the minor-suit fit will play just as well. On the 34% of deals where partner holds only four spades, you will fare much better in three of partner's minor. So, bid 2NT to ask for the minor.

On (2) you have no guarantee of an eight-card fit in a minor. Also, partner's minor (whether it is four-carded or five-carded) is more likely to be diamonds (62%) than clubs (38%). That's because you hold one more card in clubs than in diamonds. Nevertheless, in the long run it is better to play in partner's minor suit and you should again bid 2NT. Only when partner holds five spades and four diamonds will you be better off in 2♠. When, instead, partner holds four spades and a five-card minor, you will score very few matchpoints in 2♠.

On hand (3) partner's minor will be diamonds 72% of the time. It is best to pass 2♠ where your partner will hold five spades with 62% frequency. With (4) you will pass 2♠. This will be the best matchpoint contract when partner holds five spades (63%), and a playable spot when the spade fit is only 4-3.

Intervention over the Cappelletti bid

The opponents will sometimes bid over your Cappelletti intervention. This is most likely when the overcall is 2♣, showing a single-suiter:

West	North	East	South
	1NT	2♣	2◇
?			

South's 2◇ is natural. Sitting West, you can double to ask partner to bid his long suit. If instead you bid 2♡ or 2♠, this shows a good suit of your own.

West	North	East	South
	1NT	2♡	2♠
?			

Partner has shown hearts and a minor suit. Here you can play 2NT, asking partner to bid his minor. A double would be for penalties.

What difference does the vulnerability make?

The best conditions for competing against 1NT on borderline hands arise when neither side is vulnerable. If you pass, you may score badly for +50 or +100 when you could have made +110 or more. If you compete and play a contract your way, you may score well for –50 or –100 when they could have made +90, +110 or +120.

The least favorable conditions for competing arise when the opponents are vulnerable. If partner has a good hand opposite your potential Cappelletti bid and you can make +110 or +140, you will sometimes find that 1NT would have gone 200 down. When your own side is vulnerable, one down for –100 will be worse than allowing them to score +90 in 1NT. Two down for –200 is likely to be a very poor score.

So, overall, it's a great idea to shunt an opponent out of his comfortable 1NT contract, but do pay consideration to the prevailing vulnerability.

SUMMARY

- There is not much difference between the various defenses to 1NT. Choose a method that allows you to intervene as often as possible. Leaving the opponents in 1NT will often give you a poor matchpoint score.

- One effective defense to 1NT is Cappelletti. 2♣ shows a single-suiter and 2◇ shows both majors. 2♡ and 2♠ show the bid major and one of the minors. 2NT shows both the minor suits and a double is for penalties.

- All the Cappelletti bids suggest around 9-14 points.

- Your main aim is to dislodge the opponent from 1NT. Do not try for game unless you have a great trump fit. When you hold 11 points opposite a Cappelletti overcall, partner is much more likely to hold 9 or 10 points than 13 or 14.

Tᴇ⌠ᴛ Yᴏᴜʀ⌠ᴇʟ⌠

1. You are playing Cappelletti and neither side is vulnerable at matchpoints. What action will you take on these four West hands when 1NT by North is followed by two passes?

(a) ♠ K 10 8 7   (b) ♠ Q 8 7 2   (c) ♠ 9 3   (d) ♠ Q 10 3
     ♡ 9 7 3   ♡ A J 10 7 4 3   ♡ A 10 2   ♡ —
     ◊ J   ◊ 8   ◊ K Q 10 7 6 2   ◊ Q J 8 7 5
     ♣ A Q 10 7 3   ♣ Q 7   ♣ A K   ♣ K J 9 4 2

2. You are playing Cappelletti and only your side is vulnerable at matchpoints. What action will you take on these four West hands when South opens 1NT?

(a) ♠ Q J   (b) ♠ K 5 4 2   (c) ♠ K Q 8 7 3   (d) ♠ A 3
     ♡ 10 9 7 6 3 2   ♡ J 4   ♡ Q J 7 6 2   ♡ 4
     ◊ K 4   ◊ Q 10 7 6 2   ◊ 9   ◊ A Q J 8 7
     ♣ K 8 3   ♣ K 7   ♣ 10 3   ♣ K J 9 4 2

3. You are playing Cappelletti and only the opponents are vulnerable at matchpoints. What action will you take on these four West hands when you partner overcalls North's 1NT with 2◊ (showing both majors)?

(a) ♠ K 10 4   (b) ♠ 8   (c) ♠ A J 9 4   (d) ♠ A 10 3
     ♡ J 7 3   ♡ Q 4   ♡ Q 2   ♡ A Q 8 7 2
     ◊ A 10 7 3   ◊ K 10 7 6   ◊ A 10 5 3   ◊ 5
     ♣ Q 7 6   ♣ J 9 7 6 4 2   ♣ 9 7 3   ♣ 10 9 8 5

4. You are playing Cappelletti and both sides are vulnerable at matchpoints. What action will you take on these four West hands when your partner overcalls North's 1NT with 2♡ (showing hearts and a minor)?

(a) ♠ 8 4 3   (b) ♠ K J 9 6 5 4   (c) ♠ A Q 9 4   (d) ♠ J 7 3
     ♡ A 7 4   ♡ 7   ♡ J 2   ♡ 7 2
     ◊ Q 6   ◊ A 9 3   ◊ K J 5 4 3   ◊ K Q 7 6
     ♣ K J 7 6 2   ♣ J 6 5   ♣ 9 7   ♣ A Q 8 5

ANSWERS

1. On (a) you are happy to contest with 2♠, showing 4-5 or 5-4 in spades and a minor suit. With hand (b) some players might consider bidding 2◇ to show both majors. With a strong six-card suit and a moderate four-card suit, it is better to choose a major yourself. Start with 2♣ and then show a single-suiter in hearts. Hand (c) is a single-suiter in diamonds, yes, but it is too strong for a Cappelletti bid; you will begin with a double. With (d) you are a bit surprised that no one has shown hearts. Still, you know what will happen if you pass 1NT. Partner will lead a heart and wince when you show out. You can neatly side-step this situation by bidding 2NT, to show at least five cards in both minor suits.

2. Much of the time you would enter on hand (a), despite the weakness of the suit. In second seat, with the vulnerability against you, the odds tilt and you should pass. Hand (b) is also a minimum Cappelletti intervention and you would lean towards passing when vulnerable in the second seat, with a possible penalty being measured in 100s — even more if doubled. You can be bolder when you have five cards in the major or (even better) 5-5 shape. Bid 2◇ on (c). Only 8 points, yes, but 5-5 shape and all the points in the long suits. You have 15 points on (d) but if you start with a double, you can be almost certain that one of the next two players will bid a major suit. It is better to start with 2NT. This allows you to play in one of the minors, and makes it harder for your LHO to introduce a long major on a weak hand.

3. On (a) you give no thought to a game contract. The more points you hold, the more likely partner is to be at the minimum end of his potential range. Respond 2♡. (If partner was borderline for his bid, he is more likely to be 4-5 than 5-4; he expects you to bid 2♡ with equal length.) On (b) you bid 2♡, showing preference between the majors. With (c) your excellent spade fit and a potentially useful queen in partner's other suit justify a game try of 3♠. On (d) your splendid fit in both suits tells you to bid 4♡.

4. On (a) you should pass. You do not have enough for a game try. With hand (b) you are entitled to bid 2♠, suggesting that this will be the best spot. It is no certainty that you have a 5-3 fit in a minor and 2♠ is a level lower. (c) Do not bid 2NT on this hand. Remember that partner does not necessarily hold opening-bid values; indeed, the odds are against it. You should pass. (d) Bid 2NT to ask for partner's minor, and then pass. You can hardly expect to make a minor-suit game with a strong 1NT against you.

8

Lead-directing Bids and Doubles

The opening lead can be critical at IMPs. It is even more important at matchpoints, because you may need to prevent overtricks even when the contract is certain to make. We saw in Chapter 1 how you can indicate a good lead to partner by making an overcall, even perhaps a slightly risky one. In this chapter we will look at various other ways to achieve the same objective.

Lead-directing doubles during a slam auction

When the opponents are engaged in some drawn-out slam auction, this is no time to gaze out of the window. You may have the chance to double a conventional bid to suggest a good opening lead.

West	North	East	South	EAST
			1♠	♠ 8
pass	3♠	pass	4NT	♡ 10 8 6 5
pass	5◇	dbl		◇ K Q 10 5
				♣ J 9 5 3

East doubles the 5◇ Blackwood response to suggest a diamond lead.

On the next example it is a control-bid that receives this treatment:

West	North	East	South	EAST
	1◇	pass	1♠	♠ 9 2
pass	3♠	pass	4♣	♡ K 10 8 5
pass	4♡	dbl		◇ A 8 2
				♣ 8 6 4 2

The opponents agree spades as trumps. The 4♣ and 4♡ bids are then control-bids, showing the ace (or king) of the suit bid. Their purpose is to check that all the side suits are controlled. Sitting East, you expect North to hold the ♡A for his control-bid. If partner leads a heart against their eventual spade contract (perhaps 6♠), this may set up your ♡K before the ◇A is knocked out. You double 4♡ to suggest a heart lead.

Inferences when partner does not double

When partner has the chance to make a lead-directing double of a control-bid or Blackwood response and chooses not to, you may be able to draw an inference that will assist your opening lead.

(a)

West	North	East	South
	1♣	pass	1♠
pass	3♠	pass	4NT
pass	5♡	pass	6♠
all pass			

(b)

West	North	East	South
			1♡
pass	1♠	pass	4♡
pass	5♣	pass	6♡
all pass			

On auction (a) East had a chance to double 5♡ and decided against it. This will often be because he has no particular opening lead to suggest anyway. However, you know that he doesn't hold anything particularly good in hearts and he might do in diamonds! Suppose, looking at your own hand, you have no reason to choose one red suit over another. You should then prefer to lead a diamond.

Similarly, on auction (b) East had the chance to double the 5♣ control-bid, which he might well have done if he had held the ♣K. Sitting West, on lead, you are more likely to find him with something useful in diamonds than in clubs.

Lightner doubles of a freely bid slam

The great American player, Theodore Lightner, conceived the idea that a double of a freely bid slam should be lead-directing. What does 'freely bid slam' mean? It excludes those slams that are bid in a high-level competitive auction and may therefore be intended as a sacrifice.

A Lightner double asks for an unexpected lead. Often it will be based on a void in one of the side suits. If you or your partner has bid a suit, perhaps early in the auction, a lead of that suit is excluded by a Lightner double.

Let's see an example where such a double is successful.

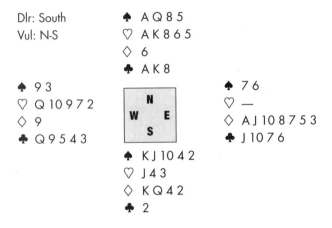

Dlr: South
Vul: N-S

North
♠ A Q 8 5
♡ A K 8 6 5
♢ 6
♣ A K 8

West
♠ 9 3
♡ Q 10 9 7 2
♢ 9
♣ Q 9 5 4 3

East
♠ 7 6
♡ —
♢ A J 10 8 7 5 3
♣ J 10 7 6

South
♠ K J 10 4 2
♡ J 4 3
♢ K Q 4 2
♣ 2

West	North	East	South
		3♢	pass
pass	dbl	pass	4♠
pass	4NT	pass	5♢
pass	6♠	dbl	all pass

When South ended in 6♠, East made a Lightner Double, hoping that partner could diagnose a heart lead. Suppose you had been West. Would you have worked out what to lead?

It was fairly clear to West that East must be void in either hearts or clubs. Since North's double had implied length in both the major suits, and he might or might not have club length, West preferred to lead a heart.

Bull's-eye! East ruffed the heart lead and cashed the ◇A for one down. After any other lead, in particular a singleton diamond lead, the slam would have been made.

Lead-directing doubles of Stayman or a transfer response

When the opponents are playing a strong 1NT, you may have the chance to double a Stayman 2♣ or a transfer response of 2◇ or 2♡ to suggest a lead. (Against a weak 1NT, it is better to use a double to show a generally strong hand, because you are more likely to have a game your way.)

(a)

West	North	East	South
	1NT	pass	2♣
dbl			

(b)

West	North	East	South
	1NT	pass	2♡
dbl			

In auction (a) West doubles on ♠873 ♡J73 ◇Q8 ♣KQ1095, to suggest a club opening lead.

On (b) the 2♡ response is a transfer bid showing at least five spades. West doubles to show that he would like a heart lead. You should not double when you hold something like ♡Q109762, just because you think 2♡ would go down. You have no particular reason to want a heart lead on that hand, particularly not from ♡Ax.

Lead-directing doubles of other artificial bids

There are plenty of other situations where the opponents' auction offers the opportunity for a lead-directing double.

(a)

West	North	East	South
			1♡
pass	1♠	pass	2◇
pass	3♣	dbl	

(b)

West	North	East	South
			1◇
pass	3◇	pass	3♡
pass	3♠	dbl	

In (a) North's 3♣ is fourth suit forcing. East doubles to suggest that a club lead will be welcome.

In auction (b) diamonds are agreed but the partnership may well want to play in 3NT. The bids of 3♡ and 3♠ are stopper bids with this aim in mind. East doubles 3♠ to show good spades sitting over North's stopper. He is inviting a spade opening lead. Remember that even if the eventual 3NT proves to be unbeatable, a spade lead may reduce the number of overtricks — critical at matchpoints.

(c)	West	North	East	South
				1◇
	dbl	pass	2◇	dbl

(d)	West	North	East	South
				1♡
	1♠	2♠	dbl	

In (c) East's 2◇ shows a strong hand and asks partner to bid suits so that a fit can be found, very possibly for a game contract. South doubles to show good diamonds, suggesting that he would like North to lead the suit.

In auction (d) North makes an artificial bid in the overcaller's suit to indicate a sound raise of partner's heart suit. East doubles to show a high card in partner's suit and to indicate that a spade lead would be welcome. Perhaps he holds ♠K5. The overcaller may then be able to make a profitable underlead of his ♠AQ763 or ♠A98642.

If, on another deal, East did not double 2♠, West would assume that the opponents held the ♠K. He would tend to look elsewhere for his opening lead.

Lead-directing doubles of a splinter bid

Suppose the opponents' bidding starts 1♠-4◇, where the response is a splinter bid showing a sound raise to 4♠ with at most one card in diamonds. What is a sensible meaning for a double of 4◇? Should it mean that you would like partner to lead a diamond?

There is unlikely to be much future in leading a suit where dummy holds only one card. The Mexican expert, George Rosenkrantz, made the clever suggestion that such a double should ask for a lead in the side suit ranked above the short suit. So a double of 4◇ would ask for a heart opening lead.

Let's see an example of this method in action.

Dlr: South
Vul: Both

Matchpoints

	♠ A Q 5 3	
	♡ A 9 5	
	◇ 4	
	♣ J 9 6 5 2	

♠ 9 8		♠ 10 6
♡ 7 6 4 3	N	♡ K Q 10 2
◇ J 10 9 7	W E	◇ A 8 5 2
♣ K 10 4	S	♣ Q 8 7

	♠ K J 7 4 2	
	♡ J 8	
	◇ K Q 6 3	
	♣ A 3	

West	North	East	South
			1♠
pass	4◇	dbl	4♠
all pass			

Sitting East, you make a Rosenkrantz double of North's splinter bid to suggest a heart lead. South signs off in 4♠ and your partner duly leads a heart. Declarer cannot avoid the loss of one trick in each side suit and you hold him to +620.

Suppose instead that West leads the ◇J. If East rises with the ◇A, declarer will ditch dummy's two heart losers on the ◇KQ. If instead East plays low, declarer will not lose a diamond trick. In both cases he will write +650 in his scorecard. After a black-suit lead, declarer can win and later play diamonds himself with the same effect. Preventing the overtrick with a heart lead may be worth half a top.

Lead-directing bids when raising a preempt

Suppose your partner's preempt has been doubled for takeout. When you have support for partner's suit and intend to raise, you may do better to bid a new suit with lead-directing intent.

(a)

West	North	East	South
	2♡	dbl	3♣

(b)

West	North	East	South
	3♡	dbl	4◇

You would not often want to compete with partner's long suit. The 3♣ and 4◇ bids should be taken as showing a single raise of partner's preempt, while suggesting a good opening lead if South ends up playing the contract. Look at this deal:

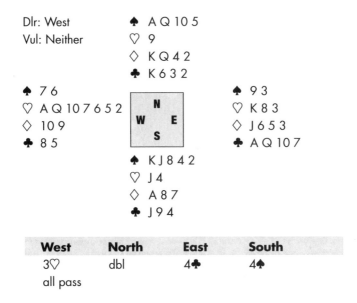

Dlr: West
Vul: Neither

North
♠ A Q 10 5
♡ 9
◇ K Q 4 2
♣ K 6 3 2

West
♠ 7 6
♡ A Q 10 7 6 5 2
◇ 10 9
♣ 8 5

East
♠ 9 3
♡ K 8 3
◇ J 6 5 3
♣ A Q 10 7

South
♠ K J 8 4 2
♡ J 4
◇ A 8 7
♣ J 9 4

West	North	East	South
3♡	dbl	4♣	4♠
all pass			

East is prepared to raise to 4♡. Suppose he takes a simple view and makes this bid. South will end as declarer in 4♠ and West will have to guess what to lead. If he chooses the ◇10 or a trump, the contract will be made.

East, who recently read a rather good book (ahem) on winning tactics at duplicate, does not bid 4♡. Instead, he bids 4♣. This would have little value in a natural sense. Instead it shows a raise to 4♡ while at the same time suggesting a club lead.

South bids 4♠, ending the auction, and West then leads a club. East pockets two club tricks and delivers a club ruff. The ♡A then puts the game one down.

Suppose that West held some different hand, very weak without the ♡A. Although 4♠ would then be cold, you might still get a near top at matchpoints by leading a club and taking the first three tricks.

Let's see a deal from top-class play (a European Open teams semifinal between Italy and France) where lead-directing mechanisms brought a handsome reward. Sitting E-W were the eighty-five-year-old Benito Garozzo (a member of the fabled Italian Blue Team) and the eighty-year-old Romain Zaleski.

```
Dlr: East          ♠ J 7 6
Vul: N-S           ♡ 7 6 4
                   ♢ Q 10 6
                   ♣ K J 9 3
♠ 4                                    ♠ 8 3
♡ Q 8 2            ┌─────────┐         ♡ K J 10 9 5 3
♢ J 7 5 3          │    N    │         ♢ A 9 8 2
♣ A Q 8 7 4        │  W   E  │         ♣ 2
                   │    S    │
                   └─────────┘
                   ♠ A K Q 10 9 5 2
                   ♡ A
                   ♢ K 4
                   ♣ 10 6 5
```

West	North	East	South
Garozzo	Lorenzini	Zaleski	Rombaut
		2♡	dbl
4♣	pass	4♢	4♠
5♡	5♠	dbl	all pass

Rombaut chose to double the weak two opening. Commentating on
Bridge Base Online, I expected Garozzo to bid 3♣ now. This would show
a raise to 3♡, while suggesting a club opening lead against a possible
spade contract played by North. Garozzo made the same sort of bid one
level higher.

Did Zaleski just bid 4♡ now? No! Realizing that South might end as
the declarer, he made a lead-directing 4♢ bid instead. South ended in 5♠
doubled and Garozzo led a diamond to his partner's ace. A club return
to the ace was followed by a club ruff, defeating the contract. Brilliant!

At the other table, Intonti for Italy overcalled 4♠ over East's opening
bid of 3♡. This allowed no space for lead-directing mechanisms, and the
eventual contract of 5♠ was made when West understandably led a low
heart.

- During an opposing slam auction the player on your right may make various artificial bids, such as a Blackwood response or control-bid. When partner is likely to be on lead, you can double one of these bids to suggest a lead of that suit.

- Against a strong 1NT, you can double a Stayman 2♣ or a transfer response of 2◇ or 2♡ to suggest the lead of the suit actually bid.

- Similarly, you can make lead-directing doubles of artificial fourth-suit-forcing bids and stopper bids during auctions heading towards 3NT.

- When your partner has bid a suit and the next player cuebids the same suit to show strength, you can double to show a high honor in the suit. Such a double will often be based on Ax or Kx. If you held greater length in partner's suit, you might raise instead.

- A double of a freely bid slam is Lightner, asking your partner to look for an unusual lead. It specifically excludes a trump or any suit that has been bid by the partnership. The doubler will often have a side-suit void and be hoping to ruff the opening lead.

- When partner's preemptive opening bid is doubled for takeout, look for the chance to make a lead-directing bid instead of a direct raise. When you hold something like AK72 or AQ83 in a side suit, partner's lead from shortage may allow you to take the first three tricks.

Test Yourself

You sit West in the bidding problems below. Assume you are using the methods advocated in this chapter.

1.
♠ 7 5
♡ 10 7 6
◇ K Q 9 8 6
♣ 9 5 4

West	North	East	South
	2♣	pass	2♠
pass	3♡	pass	4♡
pass	4NT	pass	5◇
?			

Will you double 5◇ or not?

2.
♠ 7 5
♡ J 10 7 6
◇ Q 7 6
♣ A K 5 4

West	North	East	South
		3♡	dbl
?			

Neither side is vulnerable. What action will you take?

3.
♠ 7
♡ K J 7 6
◇ 9 8 5 4
♣ K Q 10 4

West	North	East	South
	1♠	pass	4♣
?			

South's 4♣ is a splinter bid, showing a raise to 4♠ including at most one club. What action will you take?

4.
    ♠ J 7 2
    ♡ A 10 9 5 4
    ♢ —
    ♣ J 7 6 4 3

West	North	East	South
			1♢
pass	1♠	pass	3♠
pass	4NT	pass	5♡
pass	6♠	pass	pass
?			

Will you double the spade slam on these West cards?

5.
    ♠ 8 2
    ♡ K Q 10 5
    ♢ 10 8 4
    ♣ Q 7 6 2

West	North	East	South
		pass	1♢
pass	2♠	pass	3♢
pass	4♢	pass	4♡
?			

South's 4♡ cuebid presumably shows the ♡A. Will you double?

6.
    ♠ Q 9 8 3
    ♡ 10 7
    ♢ A K J 4
    ♣ 9 7 5

West	North	East	South
	1NT	pass	2♢
?			

South's 2♢ is a transfer response, showing hearts. Will you double?

ANSWERS

1. North's 5♢ is a Blackwood response and does not necessarily show the ♢A. Nevertheless, you are entitled to make a lead-directing double when holding the ♢KQ. If instead you held ♢K10764, you would not double. This might assist the opponent on your left. If he held the ♢AQ he would count this as two likely tricks and bid with more enthusiasm.

2. You are worth a defensive raise to 4♡ but it is much better to make a lead-directing bid of 4♣. You half expect North to bid 4♠ and your partner will then know you would like a club lead.

3. You should not double. Even if you were not playing Rosenkrantz doubles, it would be a waste of time to ask for a club lead when dummy holds at most one club. If you made a Rosenkrantz double, this would ask for a lead of the side suit above the splinter bid, diamonds — the last thing that you want! When you pass, instead (the correct action), partner will note that you did not ask for a diamond lead. He will be more inclined to lead a heart.

4. You should make a Lightner Double of the spade slam, asking for an unexpected lead — often one that will allow you to ruff. Leading one of the unbid suits, hearts or clubs, would not be unexpected. You are clearly asking for a diamond lead. You plan to ruff and cash the ♡A for one down. Note that it would have been a mistake to double the 5♡ Blackwood response. You want partner to lead a diamond, not a heart!

5. You should not double because you will not be on lead against a diamond contract! By doubling you would give away information with no corresponding advantage for your side. You would also give the opponents more bidding space. (The next player may make use of the option to redouble, or to pass and allow his partner to redouble — thereby indicating a first-round heart control.) Don't think that I have been a bit mean and tried to trap you with a trick question. A lot of players forget which opponent will end up as the declarer.

6. You should double 2♢ at matchpoints, since it is worth taking a slight risk to get a favorable lead. At IMPs you have to take more account of the possibility that North might redouble when holding four diamonds. If his partner held a suitable hand, they might well settle in 2♢ redoubled, possibly making with an overtrick.

9

CHOOSING THE RIGHT SLAM

What odds do you need to bid a slam such as 6♠? If you are vulnerable and the slam is not bid at the other table, you will gain 750 (1430 – 680) when the slam is successful. That will be a swing of +13 IMPs. If you attempt a slam and go one down, you will lose the same amount (100 + 650). So, at both IMPs and matchpoints, you should bid a vulnerable slam only if it is better than a 50% prospect. The odds are the same when non-vulnerable. You stand to gain 500 or lose 500.

In this chapter we will see how to choose between two different slams. At IMPs you should choose the slam that is most likely to succeed. At matchpoints, particularly when you expect a slam to be widely bid, you will look for a high-scoring slam, noting that 990 in 6NT beats 980 in a major and 920 in a minor.

Should I bid 6NT or six of a suit with a 4-4 fit?

What are the general guidelines when choosing between 6NT and a small slam in a suit where you have a 4-4 fit? A potential advantage of the 4-4 fit is that an extra trick from a ruff may bump your total from eleven tricks to twelve. When your values for a slam are minimal, it may therefore be necessary to play with a trump suit.

When you have relatively good values for a slam, there is more reason to choose 6NT. Firstly, it will score more at matchpoints. Secondly, you cannot suffer an adverse ruff that may put you down immediately. A third reason is that you may still be able to gather twelve tricks even if the suit that would otherwise be trumps happens to break badly.

Let's see some deals where these aspects are apparent.

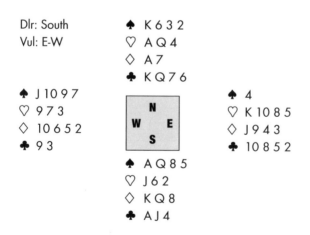

```
Dlr: South          ♠ A 10 5
Vul: Both           ♡ A Q 4 2
                    ◇ A J 8 7
                    ♣ J 6

♠ J 8 4 2              N          ♠ Q 9 7
♡ 7 3             W        E      ♡ 9 8 5
◇ 9 6 2              S          ◇ 10 4 3
♣ Q 9 3 2                        ♣ K 10 5 4

                    ♠ K 6 3
                    ♡ K J 10 6
                    ◇ K Q 5
                    ♣ A 8 7
```

West	North	East	South
			1NT
pass	2♣	pass	2♡
pass	6♡	all pass	

North has 16 points for a total of 31-33, not particularly high for a small slam on two balanced hands. He decides to play in 6♡ rather than in 6NT, in case a ruffing trick or two is needed to bring the total to twelve. As you see, there are eleven top tricks in 6NT and hardly any play for a twelfth trick. Playing in 6♡, you can give up a club and ruff a club for the twelfth trick.

Now let's make the combined holdings a bit more powerful:

```
Dlr: South          ♠ K 6 3 2
Vul: E-W            ♡ A Q 4
                    ◇ A 7
                    ♣ K Q 7 6

♠ J 10 9 7             N          ♠ 4
♡ 9 7 3           W        E      ♡ K 10 8 5
◇ 10 6 5 2           S          ◇ J 9 4 3
♣ 9 3                            ♣ 10 8 5 2

                    ♠ A Q 8 5
                    ♡ J 6 2
                    ◇ K Q 8
                    ♣ A J 4
```

West	North	East	South
			1NT
pass	2♣	pass	2♠
pass	6♠	all pass	

This time North holds 18 points, giving his side between 33 and 35 points. This should be enough for 6NT to be a good contract. But no, he decides to play in 6♠. One risk in that contract is that there could be two losers in the trump suit. South actually has quite strong trumps in this layout. Even so, the trumps break badly, giving declarer a certain loser in that suit. The heart finesse loses too (wouldn't you know it?) and the spade slam goes one down.

With 18 points opposite a strong 1NT, North should have bid 6NT. In this contract there are nine tricks outside spades, after giving up a heart, and the three top spades will bring the total to twelve. (If West held ♡Kxx or ♡Kxxx alongside his four spades, you could squeeze him for 6NT+1.)

Yes, it is only one deal and you could change a card or two and get a different result. The only real way to determine the best tactics in the long run is to use computer simulation, and we will do that next.

Should I bid Stayman on 4-4-3-2 shape, looking for a slam?

South opens a 15-17 point 1NT and you hold the North hand that we have just seen:

♠K 6 3 2   ♡A Q 4   ◇A 7   ♣K Q 7 6

Should you raise to 6NT or seek a 4-4 spade fit by bidding Stayman?

To answer this question, we will run a 5000-deal simulation where South holds a 15-17 point 1NT and would respond 2♠ to Stayman. The software will then compare the results for 6♠ and 6NT. This is the comparison:

Playing in a 4-4 spade fit, with an 18-point 4=3=2=4 North hand

Contract	Makes	Avg tricks	MPs	IMPs (V)	IMPs (NV)
6♠	85.2%	12.2	17.2%	–0.6	–0.5
6NT	89.3%	12.2	82.8%	+0.6	+0.5

The results could not be clearer. The 4-4 trump fit is rarely needed to provide a twelfth trick. Indeed, 6NT is successful more often than 6♠, where you will sometimes suffer an adverse ruff or spade losers that are unavoidable when that suit is trumps.

At matchpoints, the gulf is reminiscent of the Grand Canyon! You should not even contemplate playing a small slam in a 4-4 fit when you have a combined point count that is likely to give 6NT good play. On 67% of the 5000 deals, both 6♠ and 6NT made exactly twelve tricks and the extra +10 gave the matchpoints to the notrump slam. (On 10% of the deals, the 4-4 fit produced an overtrick in 6♠ and a swing of +20. The third most frequent result arose on the 8% of the deals where 6NT was made and 6♠ went one down.)

What is the situation when North holds only 16 points instead of 18? This will reduce the chance of 6NT making and may allow 6♠ to become the better contract (with one or more ruffing tricks available). Let's replace the ♡Q on the previous hand with the ♡7:

♠K 6 3 2   ♡A 7 4   ◇A 7   ♣K Q 7 6

Should you use Stayman now? Once again, we will compare the results for 6♠ and 6NT on 5000 deals that match the bidding:

Playing in a 4-4 spade fit, with a 16-point 4=3=2=4 North hand

Contract	Makes	Avg tricks	MPs	IMPs (V)	IMPs (NV)
6♠	70.5%	11.8	41.2%	+2.5	+2.0
6NT	56.7%	11.6	58.8%	−2.5	−2.0

Valuable information! 6NT is now much less likely to be made than 6♠ (56.7% compared to 70.5%), but it's *still* the better matchpoint contract. That's because 6NT wins the board when both slams score twelve tricks (which happens 42% of the time). At IMPs, 6♠ carries a sizeable 2.5 or 2.0 IMPs per board advantage.

Should I bid 6NT or six of a major with a 5-3 fit?

What happens when you have a 5-3 fit in a major suit? Which slam should you choose? When twelve tricks are made, 6NT gives you a vital extra 10 points over 6♠ or 6♡. How often will playing with a trump suit convert eleven tricks into twelve? Suppose you hold this South hand:

♠K 9 8 3   ♡K J 6   ◇Q J 4   ♣A J 8

West	North	East	South
			1NT
pass	2◇	pass	2♡
pass	5NT	pass	?

North's 5NT asks you to 'pick a slam'. He has shown you five hearts and declined to show a second suit on the next round. His shape is probably some variant of 5-3-3-2 and you must choose between 6♡ and 6NT. Which slam would you select at IMPs and at matchpoints?

We will wheel out our special software to generate 5000 deals that match the bidding and see which slam fares better.

Playing in a 5-3 heart fit, with 4=3=3=3 South hand

Contract	Makes	Avg tricks	MPs	IMPs (V)	IMPs (NV)
6♡	68.6%	11.8	16.8%	–0.16	–0.13
6NT	69.3%	11.8	83.2%	+0.16	+0.13

At matchpoints, 6NT wins by the biggest winning margin that we have yet seen! It scores 83.2% of the matchpoints when competing against 6♡ over the 5000 deals. 6NT wins by a much more modest margin at IMPs.

Next, we will change the opener's shape to some variant of 4-4-3-2, again with three-card heart support. Perhaps 6♡ will now be made more often than 6NT.

♠ A 4   ♡ K 8 5   ◇ A J 9 3   ♣ K 10 7 4

West	North	East	South
			1NT
pass	2◇	pass	2♡
pass	5NT	pass	?

Would you choose 6♡ or 6NT at IMPs? Which slam would you choose at matchpoints? Here are the results:

Playing in a 5-3 heart fit, with a 2=3=4=4 South hand

Contract	Makes	Avg tricks	MPs	IMPs (V)	IMPs (NV)
6♡	89.2%	12.3	10.1%	–0.36	–0.29
6NT	91.4%	12.3	89.9%	+0.36	+0.29

Both contracts make much more often. That's because the South hand has six controls (A/A/K/K) and a more productive 4-4-3-2 shape. At the slam level, the ruffing value is of little use. You will usually either have twelve tricks without it or be doomed to two losers, anyway. Indeed, 6NT is slightly more likely to make. That's mainly because you may survive a bad break in hearts. At matchpoints... wow! In a straightforward battle against the 6♡ bidders, you pick up 89.9% of the matchpoints for bidding 6NT.

Should I bid 6NT or six of a major with a 5-4 fit?

Perhaps it is right to bid 6NT even when you have a 5-4 fit. Let's see.

♠ K Q 5 ♡ A J 9 3 ◇ Q 9 6 2 ♣ K 7

West	North	East	South
			1NT
pass	2◇	pass	2♡
pass	5NT	pass	?

Once again partner has shown a 5-3-3-2 hand and the values for a slam. You now have four-card support for his hearts and a ruffing value in clubs. Will you choose 6♡ or 6NT? Here is a comparison of the results for the two contracts over 5000 deals that match the bidding:

Playing in a 5-4 heart fit, with 3=4=4=2 South hand

Contract	Makes	Avg tricks	MPs	IMPs (V)	IMPs (NV)
6♡	74.5%	11.8	20.0%	+0.62	+0.52
6NT	71.9%	11.7	80.0%	–0.62	–0.52

You could hardly wish for a clearer answer from the simulation. **You should bid 6♡ at IMPs.** The suit slam is successful slightly more often and is worth an average gain of 0.6 or 0.5 IMPs per deal. **You should bid 6NT at matchpoints**, giving yourself a better matchpoint score than 6♡ on 80% of the deals.

What conclusion should we draw from this section? At matchpoints, you should raise directly to 6NT on 5-3-3-2 shape with slam values. It is a waste of time showing the five-card major (or bidding Stayman) because you want to be in 6NT, even when partner has a four-card fit for your long suit.

Should I bid 6NT or six of a minor?

Finally, we will look at situations where you hold a long minor suit. Should you be happy with the lower-scoring minor-suit slam or place your chips on 6NT?

♠ A 4 ♡ 8 ◇ K 10 7 ♣ A J 9 8 6 4 2

West	North	East	South
			1NT
pass	?		

No doubt you have a favored method of showing long clubs. When you hold a seven-card suit, there is not much need to seek a fit. Suppose you intend to announce the final contract immediately. How would you compare 6♣ or 6NT? Or perhaps you wouldn't bid a slam with that hand. What do you think?

6♣ or 6NT, with seven-card ace-high clubs opposite 1NT

Contract	Makes	Avg tricks	MPs	IMPs (V)	IMPs (NV)
6NT	62.1%	11.5	70.8%	–1.5	–1.1
6♣	78.4%	12.0	29.2%	+1.5	+1.1

Our first answer is yes, you should bid a slam on that hand. 6♣ will make 78.4% of the time and is the right slam to bid at IMPs. 6NT makes only 62.1% of the time, but (as we have seen more than once before) it is still the right slam to bid at matchpoints.

The most common result, looking at the simulation deal by deal, is that 33% of the time both slams make twelve tricks for a difference of +70 aggregate points. 22% of the time both slams make an overtrick for a difference of +80 points. On 11% of the deals, both slams go one down and the matchpoints are shared.

The situation may change when the seven-card suit is weaker. Let's see.

♠ A 4   ♡ K 7   ◇ Q 10 8 7 5 4 2   ♣ K 6

West	North	East	South
			1NT
pass	?		

How do you fancy your slam chances now? These are the computer simulation results:

6◇ or 6NT, with seven-card queen-high diamonds opposite 1NT

Contract	Makes	Avg tricks	MPs	IMPs (V)	IMPs (NV)
6NT	51.5%	11.1	62.5%	–1.1	–0.7
6◇	58.0%	11.6	37.5%	+1.1	+0.7

A pattern is emerging. If you are going to bid a slam, you should choose the suit slam at IMPs and 6NT at matchpoints.

Note that it makes no difference if half the field decides to stop at the game-level. Since 6NT will clearly outscore both 3NT and 6◇ on the 51.5% of deals when it is successful, it must be the right contract to bid at matchpoints.

SUMMARY

- When partner opens 1NT at matchpoints and you have slam values in a balanced hand including a major suit of four or five cards, play the slam in 6NT. Do not start with Stayman or a transfer bid to look for a trump fit. Even if the suit slam will succeed more often than 6NT, the extra 10 points for 6NT will usually give you a top score.

- Choose the higher-scoring slam at matchpoints (for example, 6NT instead of 6♠) even when you expect much of the field to stop in game. All that matters is that 6NT has more than a 50% chance of succeeding.

- At IMPs, prefer to play in a suit slam if you have a nine-card trump fit, or if the values are minimal and you judge that a ruff or two may be needed.

- At both IMPs and matchpoints, you should bid a slam that you expect to be more than a 50% prospect. If you know that the slam will depend on an unavoidable finesse, do not bid it. If it seems that the slam will be on a finesse at worst but may be cold, then you should bid it.

TEST YOURSELF

1.
    ♠ K Q 7 5 2
    ♡ K Q 3
    ◇ A Q 7
    ♣ 6 4

West	North	East	South
			2NT
pass	?		

How do you plan to bid this hand opposite a 20-21 point 2NT? Would it make any difference if it was matchpoints or IMPs?

2.
    ♠ A K 7 2
    ♡ K J 7 6
    ◇ 10 9 5 4
    ♣ J

West	North	East	South
			2NT
pass	3♣	pass	3♡
pass	?		

Again, partner opens a 20-21 point 2NT. You decide to bid Stayman, let's say, and South shows a four-card (or possibly five-card) heart suit. What now? Would it make any difference whether it was matchpoints or IMPs?

3.
    ♠ J 9 8 6 5 3 2
    ♡ A 6
    ◇ A 10
    ♣ A 8

West	North	East	South
			1NT
pass	?		

How do you rate your slam chances? Would it make any difference to your bidding plan if it was matchpoints or IMPs?

ANSWERS

1. With 16 points opposite 20-21, you have enough power for 7NT. A simulation shows that this contract will be successful 93% of the time, so there is no point in seeking a spade fit of any sort. You should respond 7NT at both IMPs and matchpoints.

   (There is a 0.6% chance that an ace is missing. You should check for that if you have a mechanism available after a 2NT opening.)

2. The total point-count is 32 or 33 and you have 4=4=4=1 shape opposite a balanced hand and a known 4-4 heart fit. First, you must assess the chance of making 6NT. I was surprised when a simulation revealed that it was as high as 63%. Unless 6♥ is going to produce an overtrick fairly often, this will make 6NT the winning bid.

   Let's rerun the simulation with 6♥ as the target contract, and then compare the matchpoints and IMPs between the two possible slams. Ah, 6♥ will be successful 88% of the time and the defenders will score an average of only 0.8 tricks per deal. So, an overtrick will be made on one deal in five. Finally, we roll out the software to compare the two slams. Here is the results table:

6♥ or 6NT with a 4-4 heart fit and a 4=4=4=1 responding hand

Contract	Makes	Avg tricks	MPs	IMPs (V)	IMPs (NV)
6♥	88.5%	12.2	54.9%	+4.6	+3.9
6NT	62.6%	11.6	45.1%	–4.6	–3.9

6♥ is the better slam at matchpoints. The three most common results are: 6NT= and 6♥= (38%), 6NT= and 6♥+1 (21.4%) and finally 6NT-1 and 6♥= (20.4%). Also, 6♥ is a massive winner at IMPs because that slam is made much more often than 6NT. So, Stayman wins the day.

3.   The chance of making 6♠ is a full 85%. You don't hear the auction
      1NT–6♠ very often, but perhaps this is the moment. We must
      first take a look at 6NT. Perhaps that's a contender. Ah, 6NT
      will succeed 76% of the time, so surely it is the best matchpoint
      contract. Let's check:

6♠ or 6NT with a 7=2=2=2 responding hand

Contract	Makes	Avg tricks	MPs	IMPs (V)	IMPs (NV)
6♠	84.7%	12.2	22.9%	+1.7	+1.4
6NT	76.0%	11.9	77.1%	–1.7	–1.4

Bid 6♠ at IMPs and 6NT at matchpoints. Message received!

10

PENALTY DOUBLES AT MATCHPOINTS

When you are playing IMPs, the general advice on penalty doubles is: 'Do not double unless you think there's a fair chance of the contract going two down.' That's because you will not gain very much for one down (100 instead of 50, or 200 instead of 100). Against that, you will lose a serious number if you double them into game and they make it. The same is true if they redouble a doubled game contract and make that.

The situation is different at matchpoints, particularly when the opponents are vulnerable. If you double and get the contract just one down, you will pick up a majestic +200. This will give you a near-top on a partscore deal.

Suppose you would have scored +110 or +140, playing the contract. If vulnerable opponents outbid you, collecting only +100 for one down undoubled is likely to give you a poor matchpoint score. A penalty double will be the right move more often than you might suspect. If they go one down, your +200 will deliver a bundle of matchpoints. If, instead, they make their contract of, say, 3♠ doubled, you may find that the −140 for allowing them to make the same contract undoubled would have been a poor score, anyway.

There are no hard-and-fast rules on when you should make a penalty double. That's partly because you cannot be sure how strong the opponents' playing strength is, even if they don't hold many points. It is an area of the game where you will gradually improve your record through experience (some of it rather painful). We will look at various situations in this chapter.

Doubling after a competitive partscore auction

Let's start by looking at a typical competitive auction that arose in a matchpoint game:

```
Dlr: East        ♠ Q 10 9 5      Matchpoints
Vul: N-S         ♡ 9 7 2
                 ◇ Q 9 6 5
                 ♣ J 5

♠ 8 4 2                          ♠ 7
♡ A 8 6          N               ♡ K Q J 10 3
◇ J 10 7 2    W     E            ◇ A 8 4
♣ A 6 3          S               ♣ K 8 7 2

                 ♠ A K J 6 3
                 ♡ 5 4
                 ◇ K 3
                 ♣ Q 10 9 4
```

West	North	East	South
		1♡	1♠
2♡	2♠	3♡	3♠
dbl			

East's 3♡ is not a game try. He would bid 2NT, 3♣ or 3◇ with a possible game in mind and is merely contesting the partscore. How should you react on the West cards when South bids 3♠?

You have a fair hand for your single raise and certainly expected 3♡ to be made (for +140). Also, you have only three hearts rather than four, which increases your chances of scoring heart tricks in defense. Suppose you pass now and there is no further bidding. If South goes one down, which is quite possible from your viewpoint, you will collect only +100 and lose out to those pairs allowed to make a heart partscore. Dangerous as it may seem, you should now make a penalty double.

When the cards lie as in the diagram, declarer cannot avoid the loss of five tricks in the side suits, and you will pick up a great +200. This is worth more than any heart partscore on your cards and will be a near top. Suppose you think that South might make his contract one time in three and otherwise go one down. For every three such boards, you will collect:

+200, −730 and +200 (two near tops and one bottom)

If instead 3♠ is passed out, you will collect:

$$+100, -140 \text{ and } +100 \text{ (two poor scores and one near bottom)}$$

Suddenly, a double seems more attractive. If they make 3♠, they are likely to get a good score, anyway. Meanwhile, when 3♠ goes one down, you will pick up a barrow-load of matchpoints for your 'Magic 200'.

Now look at this situation, again with N-S vulnerable:

WEST	West	North	East	South
♠ A 8 5				1♡
♡ A 9 7	pass	2♡	pass	pass
◇ 10 8 4	dbl	pass	2♠	3♡
♣ A K 6 5	?			

Should you double now? No. You had no reason to expect 2♠ to make. It might do, it might not. You have pushed the opponents into 3♡, and if they go down you can expect to get a good matchpoint score anyway. The potential gain from a double is not worth the risk of conceding –730 for an outright bottom.

We will end this section with a deal from a Finnish Pairs final, where N-S were vulnerable:

WEST	West	North	East	South
♠ A 9 7 2		1♣	2NT	pass
♡ 5	3◇	pass	pass	3♠
◇ Q J 7 6	4◇	pass	pass	4♠
♣ K Q 8 4	?			

East's 2NT showed the red suits. West held only two certain tricks in defense (a spade and a club) and the defensive value of his partner's Unusual Notrump overcall was unknown. However, the opponents' bidding had been hesitant and it seemed that 4◇ might well have produced +130. West doubled 4♠ and was rewarded with a fine +200.

Doubling with unexpected trump tricks

Suppose the opponents follow a limited auction to a game contract and you find yourself looking at QJ108 in the trump suit. Declarer is likely to lose at least one more trump trick than he would have expected. Although no guarantee is attached, you are entitled to seek extra matchpoints with a penalty double.

This is a typical scenario:

```
Dlr: South        ♠ 10 6 2         Matchpoints
Vul: E-W          ♡ K 5 2
                  ◇ Q 10 6
                  ♣ A 9 5 3

♠ A 9 7                           ♠ 8 5 4 3
♡ Q J 10 8          N              ♡ 3
◇ 7 5           W       E          ◇ A 8 3 2
♣ J 10 6 4          S              ♣ K 8 7 2

                  ♠ K Q J
                  ♡ A 9 7 6 4
                  ◇ K J 9 4
                  ♣ Q
```

West	North	East	South
			1♡
pass	2♡	pass	3◇
pass	4♡	pass	pass
dbl	all pass		

It seems that the opponents have few values to spare when they reach game via a game try. Deciding to shift into the 'fast lane', you double on the West cards. You lead the ♣J and declarer cannot avoid the loss of two aces and two trump tricks.

On the layout shown, you collect +100 instead of +50. This would be small fry at IMPs but the matchpoint table may look like this:

N-S	E-W	Contract	By	Tricks	N-S score	E-W score	N-S MPs	E-W MPs
1	5	4♡	S	9		50	3.5	3.5
2	4	4♡(X)	S	9		100	0.5	6.5
3	7	2♡	S	9	140		6.5	0.5
4	1	4♡	S	9		50	3.5	3.5
5	6	3NT	N	8		50	3.5	3.5
6	3	4♡	S	9		50	3.5	3.5
7	8	4♡(X)	S	9		100	0.5	6.5
8	2	2♡	S	9	140		6.5	0.5

As you see, defeating 4♡ by one trick undoubled is worth only an average score of 3.5 matchpoints. The two pairs sharp enough to double the contract are rewarded with a shared top of 6.5 matchpoints.

What are the possible pitfalls of doubling a contract when you hold good trumps? Sometimes the double will warn declarer of a bad trump break and allow him to save a trick in the play — perhaps even making the contract. Another is that the opponents may run to a better contract. That's what happened on this deal:

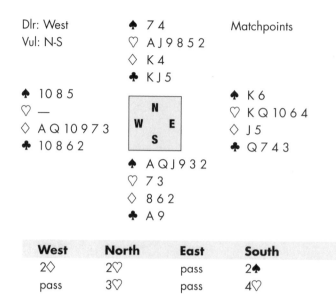

Dlr: West	Matchpoints
Vul: N-S	

```
Dlr: West        ♠ 7 4              Matchpoints
Vul: N-S         ♡ A J 9 8 5 2
                 ◇ K 4
                 ♣ K J 5
   ♠ 10 8 5                      ♠ K 6
   ♡ —              N           ♡ K Q 10 6 4
   ◇ A Q 10 9 7 3   W   E       ◇ J 5
   ♣ 10 8 6 2          S        ♣ Q 7 4 3
                 ♠ A Q J 9 3 2
                 ♡ 7 3
                 ◇ 8 6 2
                 ♣ A 9
```

West	North	East	South
2◇	2♡	pass	2♠
pass	3♡	pass	4♡
pass	pass	dbl	4♠
all pass			

With an admiring glance at his heart holding, East ventured a double of 4♡. Sensing a heart stack, South tried his luck in 4♠. There was no beating this contract and East's unwise double had misfired expensively.

Doubling after a strength-showing redouble

Many penalty doubles flow from this familiar start to an auction:

West	North	East	South
1♡	dbl	rdbl	

East tells the opener that his side holds the balance of points and he is interested in doubling for penalties the contract that N-S subsequently select. If West holds good defense against the suit that South chooses, he should not hesitate to apply a penalty double. If instead he has a sound opening bid but nothing special in the suit that South has bid, he should pass and allow his partner the option of making a penalty double. By starting with a redouble, East guarantees another bid if the opener passes.

The following deal, from the final of a North American Open Pairs, illustrates the use of a delayed strength-showing redouble.

```
Dlr: West          ♠ K 5 2
Vul: E-W           ♡ K 8 4
                   ◇ J 6 3 2
                   ♣ A 5 3
♠ Q 8 6                              ♠ A 4
♡ Q J 10 3 2          N             ♡ A 7 6
◇ A 9             W       E          ◇ 8 7 5 4
♣ K Q 8              S               ♣ 9 7 4 2
                   ♠ J 10 9 7 3
                   ♡ 9 5
                   ◇ K Q 10
                   ♣ J 10 6
```

West	North	East	South
1♡	pass	2♡	pass
pass	dbl	rdbl	2♠
pass	pass	3♡	3♠
dbl	all pass		

E-W stopped in 2♡ and North balanced with a takeout double. East, who had good defense for a single raise, indicated this with a redouble. South bid 2♠ and this ran back to East. It was not obvious to take the push to 3♡, but that is what East did. It would have turned out okay as the cards lie, with declarer losing at most a spade, a diamond and two clubs. South was not finished, however. Non-vulnerable, and hoping that his side held a 5-4 spade fit, he contested further with 3♠.

West, who had expected to make +140 in 3♡, could not afford to pick up 50s against 3♠. He doubled for penalties. The ♡Q and ♡J won the first two tricks. West continued with the ♡2, a suit-preference signal for a club switch. Declarer ruffed the third heart and ran the ♠J to East's ♠A. Back came the ♣7, a high spot card to suggest no honor in the suit. The ♣J was covered by the ♣Q, which was allowed to hold. When West continued with a fourth round of hearts, giving a ruff-and-sluff, declarer could not avoid two further losers. He was two down, N-S scoring +300 for a near-top. Had the contract not been doubled, +100 would have been a poor score.

Converting a takeout double to a penalty double

When your trumps lie under the declarer, it is dangerous to leave in a double for penalties. You should do so only when (a) your trumps have some solidity and (b) you expect the penalty to exceed what you could make your way.

Look at this instructive deal from a European mixed pairs final:

```
Dlr: South        ♠ J 9 8 7        Matchpoints
Vul: Both         ♡ 3
                  ◇ J 10 6 5 4 2
                  ♣ J 4
♠ A Q 10 4                         ♠ K
♡ 7                  N             ♡ K J 9 4 2
◇ K 9 8 3        W     E           ◇ Q 7
♣ Q 10 9 5          S              ♣ A 8 7 3 2
                  ♠ 6 5 3 2
                  ♡ A Q 10 8 6 5
                  ◇ A
                  ♣ K 6
```

West	North	East	South
			1♡
dbl	pass	pass	pass

At one table, East decided to pass for penalties. There were two things wrong with this decision. Firstly, with her trumps sitting under the declarer's holding, they would not score anywhere near as many tricks as they would when over the declarer. You need more solid trumps, something like ♡QJ1097 to consider such an action. Secondly, there was good reason to expect that E-W could score a game contract on their own cards.

West quite rightly led a trump, beginning the process of drawing trumps (if East's holding was more solid). Declarer won with the ♡8, cashed the ◇A and exited with a spade. Not long afterwards, the contract was made and N-S wrote +160 in their card.

At other tables, where the bidding started in the same way, East made the far better decision to jump to 3NT. Instead of going minus, E-W then scored +660!

Sometimes the level of the auction is fairly high and your partner competes further with a card-showing double. Although the double is basically for takeout, the best action on the hand opposite may well be to pass for penalties. That's what happened on this deal:

Dlr: South   ♠ 8 4   Matchpoints
Vul: Both   ♡ K 9 7 5 4
      ◇ J 10 4
      ♣ K 4 2

♠ A K J 9 6   ♠ Q 10 5 2
♡ J 6   **N**   ♡ Q 8 3 2
◇ 9 7 6 2 **W** **E** ◇ 3
♣ 10 3   **S** ♣ Q J 9 6

      ♠ 7 3
      ♡ A 10
      ◇ A K Q 8 5
      ♣ A 8 7 5

West	North	East	South
			1◇
1♠	dbl	3♠	dbl
all pass			

The cards did not lie particularly favorably for the defenders and their 10 points in diamonds picked up only one trick. Nevertheless, 3♠ was one down off the top and N-S collected a precious +200. No game was available their way, with the hearts breaking 4-2, so this was a near-top score.

It was clearly right for South to double at his second turn. With a powerful hand facing a negative double, he could not afford to be outbid.

SUMMARY

- At IMPs, it makes little difference if you double a contract and it goes one down. You should double only when you see some chance of two down.

- At matchpoints, a successful double may make a big difference, particularly if the opponents are vulnerable and you convert +100 into +200. You should therefore be bolder with your penalty doubles at matchpoints than at IMPs.

- The time to double at matchpoints is when you are fairly confident that you would have made your contract and it seems that the opponents are stretching to compete. As you will realize, this is not an exact science. The more sessions you play, the more experience you will gather of how aggressive you should be with your doubles.

- Double when the defensive trumps lie over the declarer's trump length.

TEST YOURSELF

All the problems below are set at matchpoints.

1. You are East, with N-S vulnerable, and the bidding starts:

♠ A 10 7 2	**West**	**North**	**East**	**South**
♡ 8 7				1♡
◇ A 8 7 2	1♠	4♡	4♠	5♡
♣ Q 5 2	pass	pass	?	

What action will you take now on this hand?

2. You are West, with both sides vulnerable, and the bidding starts:

West	**North**	**East**	**South**
1♠	dbl	rdbl	2♣
?			

What further action will you take on each of these hands?

(a) ♠ K Q 10 9 6 4	(b) ♠ A Q 8 7 2	(c) ♠ K Q J 7 5 4
♡ K J 6	♡ 9 4	♡ K 4
◇ A 8 4	◇ Q 5	◇ Q 9 6 2
♣ 8	♣ A 10 9 5	♣ 7

3. You are West, with only the opponents vulnerable. What response will you make with this hand?

♠ A 5	**West**	**North**	**East**	**South**
♡ A 10 9 8		3♣	dbl	pass
◇ J 10 6 3	?			
♣ K 4 3				

4. You are West, with neither side vulnerable. Will you take any action on this hand?

♠ A 8	**West**	**North**	**East**	**South**
♡ A 10 9		1♠	dbl	3♠
◇ 8 5 4 3	?			
♣ J 8 7 3				

ANSWERS

1. You had no reason to expect 4♠ to make. You have pushed them to the five-level and can expect to score well if 5♡ goes down, even undoubled. If 5♡ proves to be a make, though, a double from you will be costly. You may be adding an 850 to a N-S column that is sprinkled with 650s. You should pass and be happy that you have pushed them to the five-level. It is also possible that a double would allow declarer to place you with the ♢A, guessing correctly in that suit as a result.

2.(a) You are unable to double clubs yourself, but partner may wish to do so. You have a sound opening bid and should not rebid 2♠ in front of your partner. It may well be right to play the contract in spades your way. If that is what you decide, you can remove partner's penalty double of 2♣ to 2♠. Your partner will know that you have a sound opening because you did not bid 2♠ before.

  (b) Partner has suggested that the opponents should be doubled in their contract. Your good clubs justify a penalty double now. You do not need anything more than a minimum opening bid for this action. Partner's redouble has already announced that your side holds the balance of points.

  (c) Now you have a minimum hand with extra shape and little defense. You announce this by rebidding 2♠ immediately, giving partner no opportunity to make a penalty double of 2♣.

3. The deal comes from a pairs tournament in Copenhagen. Game might well have been possible in hearts or notrump, but West turned his thoughts towards defending. It was unlikely that his ♣K could be picked up, so he held three tricks in his own hand. Another three tricks from partner and that would be 500, more than a non-vulnerable game their way. Although partner held only a 5=4=2=2 12-count, the penalty was 1100. Yes, that did give E-W a top!

4. The deal comes from an ACBL Instant Matchpoint game (where you can see how many matchpoints you score immediately after you have played a deal). The best action is to double now. This is a responsive double (nominally for takeout), but you are likely to have a fairly flat hand since you have not bid a suit instead. Partner will pass out the double unless he has considerable shape of his own. The resultant +300 would have given you 86%. If instead you cautiously passed and collected only +100, you would score 17%.

11

ſACRIFICING

What does the bridge term 'sacrifice' mean? Some hopeless player asks you to partner him in the Thursday duplicate and you give up an evening that could have been more pleasurably spent elsewhere. That's one meaning. More often, your opponents bid to some contract, usually a game or a slam, and you make a higher bid even though you expect to be doubled and go down. You hope that it will cost less than allowing the opponents to make their contract.

Let's see an example of this:

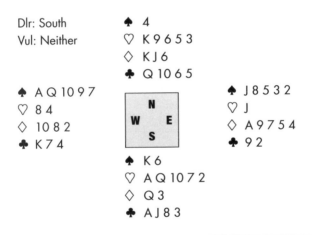

Dlr: South
Vul: Neither

North
♠ 4
♡ K 9 6 5 3
♢ K J 6
♣ Q 10 6 5

West
♠ A Q 10 9 7
♡ 8 4
♢ 10 8 2
♣ K 7 4

East
♠ J 8 5 3 2
♡ J
♢ A 9 7 5 4
♣ 9 2

South
♠ K 6
♡ A Q 10 7 2
♢ Q 3
♣ A J 8 3

West	North	East	South
			1♡
1♠	4♡	4♠	dbl
all pass			

N-S bid to 4♡ and East decides to sacrifice in 4♠. If West held good cards in both spades and diamonds, game might even be made on the E-W cards. More likely, you will go one or two down.

Here 4♠ is doubled and West escapes for one down, benefiting from the favorable position in the black suits. N-S collect only 100 instead of the 420 that would have come their way in 4♡, so 4♠ was a 'good sacrifice'.

Suppose the cards lay differently and North held the ♣A. Now 4♠ doubled would go two down. It would still be a good sacrifice, losing 300 instead of 450.

This table shows how many IMPs are scored by the sacrificing side when 4♡ is allowed to play at the other table.

Sacrificing at IMPs (Neither side vulnerable)

	4♠X=	4♠X–1	4♠X–2	4♠X–3	4♠X–4
4♡=	+14	+8	+3	–2	–9
4♡–1	+11	–4	–8	–11	–13

As you see, you can lose a significant number of IMPs against a making 4♡ only when you go four or more down. The big losses are more likely to come when 4♡ would have gone down.

The effect of vulnerability on sacrificing at IMPs

When you are vulnerable, the cost of going down in a sacrifice mounts more steeply (–200, –500, –800, –1100, etc). When you set these against the cost of a making game by non-vulnerable opponents (around –420), you see that you will gain only when you escape for one down. This (rather discouraging) table shows the potential fate of sacrificing when vulnerable against non-vulnerable.

Sacrificing at IMPs (Vulnerable against non-vulnerable)

	4♠X=	4♠X–1	4♠X–2	4♠X–3	4♠X–4
4♡=	+15	+6	–3	–8	–12
4♡–1	+12	–6	–11	–13	–15

So, you should sacrifice only when you hope to escape for one down. If you happen to go two down, though, this will cost only 3 IMPs against a making 4♡.

When you are non-vulnerable and the opponents have just bid to a vulnerable game, the odds are at their most favorable for sacrificing. The possible outcomes in IMPs are fairly enticing:

Sacrificing at IMPs (Non-vulnerable against vulnerable)

	4♠X=	4♠X–1	4♠X–2	4♠X–3	4♠X–4
4♡=	+15	+11	+8	+3	–5
4♡–1	+10	–5	–9	–12	–14

When their 4♡ would have made, your sacrifice in 4♠ will gain IMPs unless you go four down or more. If you can escape for one or two down, you will pick up a very worthwhile swing.

Finally, we will look at the situation when both sides are vulnerable:

Sacrificing at IMPs (Both sides vulnerable)

	4♠X=	4♠X–1	4♠X–2	4♠X–3	4♠X–4
4♡=	+16	+9	+3	–5	–10
4♡–1	+12	–7	–12	–14	–15

So, one down is a big pick-up of 9 IMPs. Two or three down is a moderate swing one way or the other. You would not generally sacrifice if you expected to go two down, because the most you could gain would be 3 IMPs and you might lose a bundle if their game was going down. The same is true if your other pair happened to stop short of 4♡ for some reason.

Indications that you should sacrifice

Judging well in potential sacrifice situations is no easy matter, it has to be admitted. Even experts find it difficult and some of them have a lifetime's experience in such matters. Even so, there are some pointers that encourage you to sacrifice. What do you make of this situation?

Vul: N-S

West		West	North	East	South
♠ 10 8 2				1♡	1♠
♡ Q 7		pass	2♡	3♣	4♠
◇ Q 8 7 2		?			
♣ 10 8 7 3					

North's 2♡ showed a sound raise in spades. How do you assess the potential sacrifice in 5♣? Take a while to consider the matter before you continue reading.

Perhaps you think that your hand is nothing special in support and that 5♣ could go for a big penalty. It's not the right assessment. These factors suggest that you should sacrifice:

·   The opponents are vulnerable and you are not
·   The opponents' auction was very confident. You have no surprise for them in defense and can expect 4♠ to make.
·   If it is matchpoints, the confident auction suggests 4♠ will be widely bid.

- Partner will surely be (at least) 5-5 in his suits. You have four-card support for his clubs and a very useful doubleton ♡Qx to help him to establish the hearts.

Although one deal proves nothing, here is the original layout, which arose in an IMPs match:

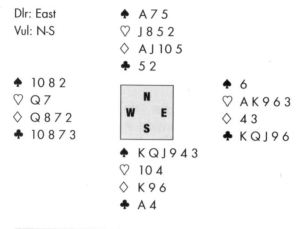

Dlr: East	♠ A 7 5
Vul: N-S	♡ J 8 5 2
	◇ A J 10 5
	♣ 5 2

West hand: ♠ 10 8 2 ♡ Q 7 ◇ Q 8 7 2 ♣ 10 8 7 3

East hand: ♠ 6 ♡ A K 9 6 3 ◇ 4 3 ♣ K Q J 9 6

South hand: ♠ K Q J 9 4 3 ♡ 10 4 ◇ K 9 6 ♣ A 4

West	North	East	South
		1♡	1♠
pass	2♡	3♣	4♠
5♣	dbl	all pass	

The sacrifice cost 300, and at the other table South scored +650 in 4♠. (Declarer finessed West for the ◇Q because East had shown length in hearts and clubs.) This was a swing of 8 IMPs to the West who diagnosed the 5♣ sacrifice.

The most important thing that West had to do was to visualize partner's hand. His own hand was pretty sad, but he should have known that it would combine well with the cards that East's bidding had suggested.

Sacrificing at matchpoints

At matchpoints, as always, you are not concerned with the size of your score. All that matters is that you beat as many of the other pairs as possible, even it is by a small margin.

Suppose no one is vulnerable and your opponents bid to 4♡, which will give you −420 if it is made. Should you sacrifice in 4♠, which you expect to cost −300? In general, you should. But if their game was bid on borderline values, there are two possible outcomes that will not favor you. Firstly, their game may go down. Secondly, their game may not be bid at some of the other tables. Losing 300 will give you a worse score than the rival pairs who concede 170 to a partscore.

Such matters are difficult to judge and this is one of the attractions of bridge. If it was an easy game, where a good player would always make the right decisions, it would be much less enjoyable.

Let's look at a typical sacrifice deal from a real-life club game. Take the South cards here:

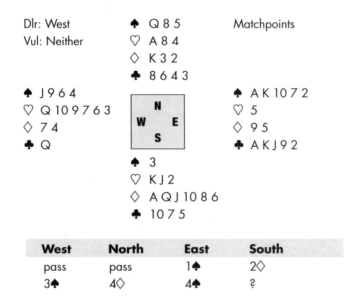

West	North	East	South
pass	pass	1♠	2◇
3♠	4◇	4♠	?

Looking only at the South cards for the moment, would you sacrifice in 5◇?

At more than one table, South did bid 5◇ and was doubled by East. The defense scored four tricks in the black suits and declarer eventually had to finesse the ♡J. When this lost to the ♡Q, the penalty was 500, more than the possible 420 if East had made 4♠.

'That was unlucky,' exclaimed South. 'If the heart finesse had won, it would have been a good sacrifice.'

Let's take a look at the scoresheet for this board:

N-S	E-W	Contract	By	Tricks	N-S score	E-W score	N-S MPs	E-W MPs
1	7	5◇X	S	8		500	0.5	6.5
2	6	4♠	E	9	50		6	1
3	2	4♠	E	10		420	2.5	4.5
4	4	5◇	S	8		150	4	3
5	3	4♠	E	10		420	2.5	4.5
6	1	4♠	E	9	50		6	1
7	8	5◇X	S	8		500	0.5	6.5
8	5	5♠	E	10	50		6	1

A mixed bag of results, as is often the case. As you see, escaping for 300 in 5◇ doubled (on some different lie of the cards) would not necessarily have been a 'good sacrifice'. Only two E-W pairs made the spade game. (They doubtless finessed North for the ♠Q, on the basis that South was likely to hold six diamonds to North's three.)

That's one point to remember, then. Sacrificing for less than the opponents' game contract will only give you a good matchpoint score if (a) most pairs sitting in the other direction bid game, and (b) most of them make the game.

There is one other lesson we can draw from this scoresheet. Look what happened to E-W Pair 4. Their opponents sacrificed in 5◇ and they did not double them! This resulted in a score of only +150 for three down; E-W scored 3 MPs instead of 6.5 MPs. It is essential to double the opponents when they sacrifice against you. Don't worry that their contract will occasionally be made. If this happens, it would usually have been a poor board for you even without a double. Think instead of the additional penalty that you will collect most of the time. Scoring +300 instead of +100, for example, can be worth a bundle of MPs.

The advance sacrifice

Sometimes you leap to a sacrifice contract before the opponents have had a chance to judge what they can make under their own steam. The objective, as so often in competitive auctions, is to remove the opponents' bidding space. Look at this example from the final of the 2013 European Open Pairs:

Dlr: South
Vul: N-S

	♠ 8 6 5 4 2	Matchpoints
	♡ 10	
	◇ K 7 5	
	♣ 9 7 3 2	

♠ 10 7		♠ —
♡ A K 7 4 3	N	♡ Q J 9 6 2
◇ J 4 3 2	W E	◇ 10 9 6
♣ 6 5	S	♣ K Q J 10 4

	♠ A K Q J 9 3	
	♡ 8 5	
	◇ A Q 8	
	♣ A 8	

West	North	East	South
			2♣
2♡	pass	5♡	dbl
all pass			

South opened with a strong 2♣. Not subdued by this, West overcalled 2♡. At the very least, the bid would suggest a good opening lead if North ended as declarer.

What should East bid now? You can see what a poor effort a raise to 4♡ would be. South could bid 4♠ and North would then be able to compete with 5♠ over a possible 5♡ from one of the opponents. East made an advance sacrifice of 5♡ and this did, indeed, cause a problem for South.

With five potential losers in his hand, he decided against bidding 5♠. He doubled and the defenders collected four tricks for a penalty of +300. E-W scored 34 MPs out of 44 MPs on the board.

SUMMARY

- At IMPs, you gain relatively little by sacrificing for 500 against the opponents' possible 620 in 4♠ — just 3 IMPs. If 4♠ goes down at the other table, or is not bid, losing 500 can be very expensive. So, do not sacrifice at IMPs unless you see a chance of scoring a fair-sized swing.

- At matchpoints, a 500 sacrifice against a string of opposing 620s may give you a wonderful score. It will do so only if several conditions apply:

  - game is widely bid on the opponents' cards,
  - game is widely made,
  - you do not go more down than you expected.

  So, when the decision appears to be borderline (even to a tiger such as yourself!), err on the cautious side.

- The vulnerability is a prime consideration. You can afford to go three down when only the opponents are vulnerable. You can afford to go only one down, when you are vulnerable and the opponents are not.

- It is rarely right to bid 'five over five'. If the opponents go to 5♡ in a competitive auction, it is usually right to pass or double, rather than stretching to 5♠.

TEST YOURSELF

1. Neither side is vulnerable. What will you bid on this hand? (Consider if your choice would vary between IMPs and matchpoints.)

WEST	West	North	East	South
♠ Q 7 6 3			2♠	pass
♡ J 6	?			
◇ 10 9 3				
♣ A 10 6 2				

2. Only N-S are vulnerable. What will you say next on this hand? (Consider if your choice would vary between IMPs and matchpoints.)

WEST	West	North	East	South
♠ A 9 4 3			3♠	4♡
♡ 8 3	4♠	5♡	pass	pass
◇ A Q 8 4	?			
♣ 9 5 2				

3. Only N-S are vulnerable. What will you bid on this hand? (Consider if your choice would vary between IMPs and matchpoints.)

WEST	West	North	East	South
♠ 6		1♡	dbl	4♡
♡ 7 6 3	?			
◇ J 9 3 2				
♣ A 10 8 6 3				

ANSWERS

1. Sweden's Sandra Rimstedt held this hand facing France in the Women's World Championship. Expecting that the opponents could make game somewhere, she bid 4♠ (an advance sacrifice). The French North did not like to double on ♠AK5 ♡A8 ◇KQJ87 ♣KQ3, since this would be primarily for takeout. (Her partner held 0=6=3=4 shape and would have bid 5♡, going one down.) 4♠ was passed out and went two down for −100, but the expected 4♠ doubled would have been a good sacrifice anyway. The French East did not open 2♠ at the other table, Sweden bidding and making 4♡.

2. By bidding to 4♠, you and your partner have already made life difficult for the opponents. What are their prospects in 5♡, would you say? Maybe eleven tricks can be made (for 650) and maybe you can escape for 500 or even 300 in 5♠. Yes, but you should not go to 5♠ now. Be happy that the opponents are at the five-level. If they are too high, it will be a good board for you. If the cards lie differently (one of them is void in spades and the diamonds lie well for them) they may be able to make 6♡. On hands such as this it is rarely right to bid 'five over five.' You should lead the ♠A. Perhaps this is the full diagram:

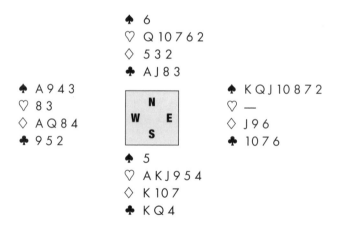

If you fail to cash the ♠A, declarer will ditch his spade on the clubs, ruff dummy's ♠6 and escape for just two diamond losers with an elimination play. (On a different lie, you might need to lead a *low* spade for a diamond return!)

3. What are the prospects for 4♡? A spade ruff or two might beat it, but you are not on lead. It's no certainty, but the contract is likely to succeed. Your three-card heart holding tells you that partner will have at most one heart loser. A sacrifice in a minor suit will be cheap so you should bid an Unusual 4NT, asking partner to choose a minor suit. With equal length in the minors, he will choose clubs.

PART TWO

DUMMY PLAY TACTICS

12

$\int$HOULD I MAKE A $\int$AFETY PLAY?

When you are playing IMPs, you should generally look for the safest way to make the contract. An overtrick is worth relatively little and you must try to ensure the game or slam bonus.

The situation is very different at matchpoints. An overtrick may then be worth a substantial amount, sometimes half a top, and it is often right to ignore an available safety play. Suppose it would give you the contract on the 20% of deals where you encounter a bad break, surrendering an overtrick on the other 80%. Taking the safety play would then give you four bad matchpoint scores for every good one!

An example will make this clear:

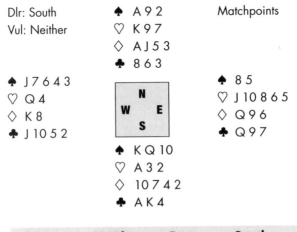

Dlr: South
Vul: Neither

```
          ♠ A 9 2          Matchpoints
          ♡ K 9 7
          ◇ A J 5 3
          ♣ 8 6 3
♠ J 7 6 4 3              ♠ 8 5
♡ Q 4            N       ♡ J 10 8 6 5
◇ K 8        W      E    ◇ Q 9 6
♣ J 10 5 2       S      ♣ Q 9 7
          ♠ K Q 10
          ♡ A 3 2
          ◇ 10 7 4 2
          ♣ A K 4
```

West	North	East	South
			1NT
pass	3NT	all pass	

You reach 3NT, which will surely be a universal contract. How should you play when West leads the ♠4?

You have eight top tricks, so one extra trick from the diamond suit will give you the game. What play in the diamond suit would guarantee you a second diamond trick, however the cards lie?

The safety play is to lay down the ◇A on the first round. You then lead towards the ◇10 (or towards the ◇J) on the second round. Even if one of the defenders started with ◇KQ984, you would make your game-going trick with the ◇10 or ◇J. If instead you begin by leading low to the ◇J, you would go down in 3NT when East held a singleton ◇K or ◇Q.

At IMPs, you should use this safety play, guaranteeing the contract. What line should you follow at matchpoints? You should lead a low diamond to the ◇J on the first round. You will go down when East holds a singleton honor, yes, but this is only a 6% chance. Leading to the ◇J will give you three diamond tricks (for an overtrick) when West holds ◇Kx, ◇Qx or ◇KQx. By spurning the safety play, you will pick up five good scores for every bad score.

Dlr: South　　　♠ 9 7 2　　　Matchpoints
Vul: Neither　　♡ A K Q 8 6
　　　　　　　　◇ 4 2
　　　　　　　　♣ 6 5 4

♠ J 10 6 4　　　　　　　　　　　♠ Q 8 5
♡ J 5　　　　　　　N　　　　　♡ 10 9 3 2
◇ Q J 10 8 6　　W　　E　　　◇ 9 3
♣ J 8　　　　　　　S　　　　　♣ K Q 9 7

　　　　　　　　♠ A K 3
　　　　　　　　♡ 7 4
　　　　　　　　◇ A K 7 5
　　　　　　　　♣ A 10 3 2

West	North	East	South
			1◇
pass	1♡	pass	2NT
pass	3NT	all pass	

Here's another one. How will you play 3NT when West leads the ◇Q?

You start with eight top tricks and will look to the heart suit to increase this total. At IMPs, where the prime consideration is to make the contract as often as possible, you would immediately duck a round of hearts. This would allow you to score four heart tricks (for a total of nine tricks) whenever the suit breaks no worse than 4-2. You are not worried by the fact that if hearts divide 3-3 you could have scored an extra 30 points by playing hearts from the top. Now, how should you play the contract at matchpoints?

To answer this question, you need to know the probability of a 3-3 heart break. It's about 36%. Suppose you decide to try for a precious overtrick, playing the heart suit from the top. 36% of the time you will score +430 for a fine score. When hearts do not break 3-3, you're likely to go down and pick up a minus score. If instead you take the safety play of ducking a heart, you will score +400 when hearts break 4-2. On 48% of the deals you will beat the declarers who play hearts from the top. In the long run, you will gain handsomely by taking the safety play.

You face a similar situation on the next deal. First, you must decide what safety play to employ at IMPs. Secondly, you need to calculate whether that is the right line of play at matchpoints. Over to you!

```
Dlr: South          ♠ 10 7 4        Matchpoints
Vul: E-W            ♡ 7 3
                   ◇ A 10 9 2
                   ♣ J 8 7 2

♠ K 8 3                          ♠ Q 9 5 2
♡ Q J 10 8 5        N            ♡ 6 4 2
◇ 8 4 3         W       E        ◇ K 7 6
♣ K 9              S             ♣ 6 4 3

                   ♠ A J 6
                   ♡ A K 9
                   ◇ Q J 5
                   ♣ A Q 10 5
```

West	North	East	South
			2NT
pass	3NT	all pass	

West leads the ♡Q. Playing IMPs, how would you give yourself the best chance of making the contract?

You duck the first round of hearts and win the heart continuation. Suppose your next move is to run the ◇Q. East will win and clear the heart suit. When a subsequent club finesse loses, West will claim two more heart tricks for one down.

On such deals you should aim to knock out first the stopper held by the danger hand (West here). Provided West holds at least four hearts, which is a huge odds-on shot after his lead in the suit, you can guarantee the contract by playing the ace and queen of clubs first, instead of taking the diamond finesse. Whichever defender wins (it will be West here), you take the heart continuation and then run the ◇Q into the safe hand. In the dangerous case where hearts break 5-3, East will have no heart to return.

So, that is the way to play the contract at IMPs. Take a moment to consider whether you should play any differently at matchpoints.

The best line at matchpoints is to take both minor-suit finesses, even though this risks going down when both finesses lose and West began with five hearts. The following tables give you the number of tricks that you will make on the two possible lines when West holds five hearts:

Taking two finesses	◇K onside	◇K offside		Using the safety play	◇K onside	◇K offside
♣K onside	11	10		♣K onside	10	9
♣K offside	10	8		♣K offside	10	9

In rough terms, taking both finesses will give you a better matchpoint score 50% of the time — when the ♣K is onside. (When you take the safety play, you regain a small bit of the lost ground if you drop a singleton ♣K offside, but this is less than a 3% chance.)

Taking two finesses will give you a worse matchpoint score only around 25% of the time (when both kings are offside). Clearly, you should take both finesses at matchpoints.

You may think that the odds swing even more in favor of taking two finesses, since hearts may be 4-4. Yes, but in that case, East may switch to a spade instead of clearing the hearts. The defenders can then still score five tricks when both minor-suit finesses fail.

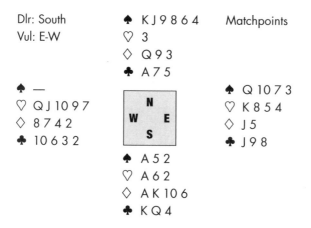

```
Dlr: South        ♠ K J 9 8 6 4      Matchpoints
Vul: E-W          ♡ 3
                  ◇ Q 9 3
                  ♣ A 7 5

♠ —                              ♠ Q 10 7 3
♡ Q J 10 9 7                     ♡ K 8 5 4
◇ 8 7 4 2        N               ◇ J 5
♣ 10 6 3 2     W   E             ♣ J 9 8
                 S
                  ♠ A 5 2
                  ♡ A 6 2
                  ◇ A K 10 6
                  ♣ K Q 4
```

West	North	East	South
			2NT
pass	3♡	pass	3♠
pass	5♠	pass	6♠
all pass			

North shows his spades with a transfer response and invites a slam with 5♠. Although you hold a minimum 20 points and an unproductive 4-3-3-3 shape, you like the look of those top cards and bid 6♠. How will you play the slam when West leads the ♡Q?

The two hands fit like a dream and the slam is a magnificent one. You have no losers in the side suits, so the only risk is that you will lose two trump tricks. Suppose first that you are playing IMPs. Many players would lay down the ♠A, gasping at their bad luck when West showed out and they had to lose two trump tricks. It's not the right play! At IMPs, you should start with a low spade from the South hand. When West shows out, you rise with dummy's ♠K and lead back the ♠J (or ♠9), planning to run the card. If East covers, you win with the ♠A and force out East's remaining remaining honor to make the slam. Suppose instead that West follows with a spotcard on the first round. You will rise with dummy's king and continue with ace and another if East shows out.

How should you play 6♠ at matchpoints? Should you take the safety play or start with the ♠A? In general, you should play as safely as possible any game or slam that you do not expect to be widely bid. That's because an overtrick may be worth relatively little and to go down would be costly.

On this particular deal, the safety play just described (king first, and then low to the ace unless West shows void) is as good as anything in terms of seeking a good matchpoint score. You will score an overtrick against the 2-2 breaks and singleton ♠Q on both sides. Starting with the ♠A, intending to finesse the ♠J on the second round, would score an overtrick when West began with Qxx (19%) or Q10xx (5%). It would lose an overtrick when East has Qx (20%) and cost the contract when East has Q10xx (5%).

Most players don't make detailed calculations. They have a general feeling of the odds and play accordingly. They may think, 'Wow, this is a great slam. Lots of pairs will miss it, so I'd better not risk going down!'

Testing whether the safety play is necessary

Sometimes it is possible to check if a safety play is necessary. This is eminently desirable at matchpoints, because you can then score the maximum possible number of tricks, whether the key suit breaks or not.

Dlr: South ♠ 7 2 Matchpoints
Vul: Both ♡ J 6 4
◇ A K Q 8 3
♣ 6 3 2

♠ J 9 8 5 3   ♠ K 10
♡ Q 9 2   ♡ K 10 8 3
◇ 9   W   E   ◇ J 10 7 5
♣ J 9 7 4   S   ♣ Q 10 5

♠ A Q 6 4
♡ A 7 5
◇ 6 4 2
♣ A K 8

West	North	East	South
			1NT
pass	3NT	all pass	

West leads the ♠5 against your contract of 3NT and you win East's ♠K
with the ♠A. Counting two tricks in spades now, you can see eight top
tricks. If diamonds break 3-2, two further diamond tricks are available
and you can make an overtrick. If the diamond suit is divided 4-1, you
would need to duck the first or second round of diamonds to score your
game without an overtrick. How should you tackle the play?

At Trick 2, you play a diamond to the ace, both defenders following.
Should you now duck the second round of diamonds? No, because the
odds at the moment favor a 3-2 break and at matchpoints you cannot
afford to miss out on the potential overtrick. Instead, you should return
to your hand with the ♣A and lead a second round of diamonds from
your hand. If West were to follow suit, you would win in the dummy and
hope for a 3-2 break. (At IMPs you would duck instead, as a safety play
against a 4-1 break.) When the cards lie as in the diagram, West will
show out. You then know, in good time, that it is essential to duck the
second round of diamonds. You will score +600 and beat those declarers
who carelessly play diamonds from the top and go down.

How the odds shift

The odds in favor of a safety play in a suit may shift when information becomes available on the lie of the other suits. Look at this deal:

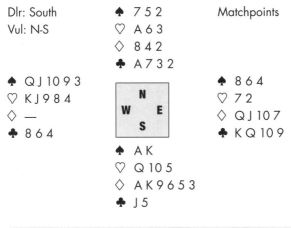

Dlr: South
Vul: N-S

♠ 7 5 2
♡ A 6 3
♢ 8 4 2
♣ A 7 3 2

Matchpoints

♠ Q J 10 9 3
♡ K J 9 8 4
♢ —
♣ 8 6 4

♠ 8 6 4
♡ 7 2
♢ Q J 10 7
♣ K Q 10 9

♠ A K
♡ Q 10 5
♢ A K 9 6 5 3
♣ J 5

West	North	East	South
			1♢
2♢	pass	2♠	2NT
pass	3NT	all pass	

West ventures a Michaels cuebid, showing at least 5-5 shape in the majors. He leads the ♠Q against your contract of 3NT and you can see ten top tricks for +630 if diamonds break 2-2. If they are 3-1, you can surrender a diamond trick for +600. How about a 4-0 diamond break?

Only East can hold all four missing diamonds. If he does, you can still make the contract with a safety play. You lead low to the ♢8 at Trick 2, subsequently taking two finesses in the suit. So, should you guard against a 4-0 diamond break with this safety play, giving up the potential overtrick when diamonds are 2-2? What do you think?

In the absence of any opposition bidding, the chance of a 2-2 diamond break would be around 40%, compared to just a 5% chance of East holding all four missing diamonds. A safety play would give you eight bad scores for every one good score, and you would not consider it at matchpoints. Here, West has announced considerable length in the majors and the odds shift. A computer simulation shows that the chance of a 2-2 diamond break drops to 22%, while there is a full 25% chance of East holding all four diamonds! You should therefore take the safety play even at matchpoints.

SUMMARY

- The usual aim of a safety play is to guarantee the contract against a bad break. This makes good sense when playing IMPs. At matchpoints, you often cannot afford to make the safety play since this may cost you a valuable overtrick when the bad break does not arise.

- If you are in a contract that you expect to be widely bid, do not take a safety play if the potentially threatening bad break is appreciably less than a 50% chance.

- Bear in mind that the odds in one suit will shift considerably when a bad break becomes apparent in some different suit.

TEST YOURSELF

1.
         ♠ 9 5
         ♡ J 6
         ◇ 9 8 4
         ♣ A K Q 7 6 2
         ━━━━━
         ♠ A K 7 3
         ♡ Q 7 3
         ◇ A K 7 5
         ♣ 8 4

West leads the ♠4 against 3NT, East playing the ♠J. How will you play the contract (a) at IMPs and (b) at matchpoints?

2.
         ♠ A Q J
         ♡ 9 5 3
         ◇ A J 6 2
         ♣ K Q 8
         ━━━━━
         ♠ K 4
         ♡ A Q 7 6 4 2
         ◇ Q 10 4
         ♣ A 6

West leads the ♣10 against 6♡. How will you play the contract (a) at IMPs and (b) at matchpoints?

3.
         ♠ 7 6
         ♡ A K J 6
         ◇ 5 4 3
         ♣ K J 6 4
         ━━━━━
         ♠ A Q 9
         ♡ Q 7 5
         ◇ A Q
         ♣ A Q 10 9 2

After bidding of 2NT–4NT–6NT, West leads the ♡9. How will you play the slam (a) at IMPs, and (b) at matchpoints?

ANSWERS

1.(a) You have seven top tricks. At IMPs you should duck the first round of clubs, so that you can make five club tricks (and the contract) when clubs break 4-1.

  (b) You cannot afford this safety play at matchpoints. Clubs will break 3-2 68% of the time, so you should play clubs from the top. This will give you a valuable overtrick nearly seven times out of ten. Remember that at matchpoints the frequency of the gain is the important measure. The fact that you will score only another 30 for the overtrick and lose the whole game bonus when clubs fail to break 3-2 is irrelevant.

2.(a) The potential losers in the diamond suit can be discarded on the surplus winners in the black suits, so all will depend on your chosen play in the trump suit. If East holds ♡Kx, a finesse of the ♡Q will net you an overtrick. A safety play is available: cash the ♡A first, to avoid defeat when West holds a singleton ♡K. If the king does not fall, you enter dummy to lead towards the ♡Q on the second round. Clearly, you should maximize your chance of making the slam at IMPs by employing this safety play.

  (b) At matchpoints, the situation is different. With a 6-3 trump fit and a combined count of 32 HCPs, you can expect most of the field to be in a slam. You cannot afford to ignore the solid 20% chance of making an overtrick. The safety play would reward you (by dropping a singleton ♡K offside) on only 6% of deals.

3.(a) Provided West has no more than three hearts, you can guarantee the contract. After removing West's hearts and clubs, you play a spade to the nine. West wins with the ♠J or ♠10, let's say, but will then have to lead into one of your AQ tenaces. The slam is yours.

  (b) In a matchpoint pairs, should you be tempted to take the spade and diamond finesses, instead, seeking an overtrick? No! The occasions when East holds both kings and you score a top for your overtrick would be cancelled out by the times when West held both kings and you went down. Apart from that, you will get a fine pairs score for making twelve tricks in 6NT, beating all the pairs in 6♣ or a game contract.

13

Recovering from a Bad Start

Sometimes at matchpoints an opponent makes an inspired opening lead against you. Whether or not the contract is destined to make, you are worried that the successful opening lead will leave you with a trick fewer than your rival declarers. Alternatively, you may have ended in a poor contract, one that threatens to give you a lower score than is being gathered elsewhere.

In adverse circumstances such as these, you must be willing to play adventurously to recover the situation. Perhaps there is a finesse that would normally be too dangerous. You may need to risk that finesse in an effort to regain the ground that you have lost.

Recovering from a hostile opening lead

If the opponents have found a lucky opening lead, one that you expect to be found at few other tables, you may need to launch a rescue operation. Look at this matchpoints deal:

```
Dlr: South        ♠ A Q 8           Matchpoints
Vul: Both         ♡ Q 5 2
                  ◇ J 10 6 3
                  ♣ 6 5 2

♠ K 7 6 4              N            ♠ J 10 9 5 3
♡ 8 3                              ♡ 7 6
◇ A 7 5 2        W        E        ◇ 9
♣ K 9 7              S             ♣ Q J 10 4 3

                  ♠ 2
                  ♡ A K J 10 9 4
                  ◇ K Q 8 4
                  ♣ A 8
```

West	North	East	South
			1♡
pass	2♡	pass	4♡
all pass			

West leads the ◇A against 4♡, continuing with a low diamond ruffed by East. You survey the scene in disbelief. How did he find that lead? You win the ♣Q return with the ♣A and draw trumps in two rounds. What now?

You expect that few West players will find such a diabolical lead. The other declarers will score one more trick than you unless you can recover in some way. Fortunately, there is a chance of doing this. You can take the spade finesse. It will risk the contract, of course, but if the finesse wins you will be able to discard your club loser. You may retrieve something close to an average score.

What would happen if the ♠Q lost to the ♠K by East? You would get the same bottom score that would be yours if you hadn't taken the spade finesse. Scoring ten tricks would be no good against the eleven tricks recorded by most of the field. By taking the spade finesse, you have much to gain and little to lose.

West found an inspired opening lead on the next deal, too:

Dlr: South   ♠ Q 6 5   Matchpoints
Vul: N-S   ♡ Q 10 9 5
         ◇ A J 6 5
         ♣ J 3

♠ K 7   ♠ A 9 8 4 2
♡ 7 6 2   N   ♡ 3
◇ 10 9 7   W   E   ◇ Q 3
♣ K Q 9 7 4   S   ♣ 10 8 6 5 2

        ♠ J 10 3
        ♡ A K J 8 4
        ◇ K 8 4 2
        ♣ A

West	North	East	South
			1♡
pass	3♡	pass	4♡
all pass			

You bid to 4♡ and West makes the somewhat wild opening lead of the
♠K. East plays an encouraging ♠9, wins the next spade with the ace and
gives his partner a spade ruff. Just your luck! How will you play the
hand when West then switches to the ♣K?

To make your game, you need to avoid a diamond loser. At IMPs
(or at a one-table home game), you would take the percentage play in
diamonds, cashing the ◇K and then finessing the ◇J.

Is the same play right at matchpoints after the start that you have
had? No! Suppose West does hold ◇Qxx and you pick up the diamond
suit. You will make ten tricks, yes, but it will be a near bottom. Those
declarers who did not suffer the outrageous spade lead will then make
eleven tricks, just losing two spade tricks. Your only chance to catch up
with the other declarers is to play the diamond suit in a different way —
playing to drop the ◇Q in the East hand.

After drawing trumps, you play the ◇A and ◇K. When the ◇Q falls
from East, you will pick up +620 and an average board. What if West
held ◇Qxx and you went two down? It would cost you almost nothing!
Once the defenders had scored the first three tricks, you couldn't possibly
have equaled the +650 scored by the other declarers.

Many players are reluctant to choose a trump as their opening lead. On the next deal, unfortunately for you, the guy on lead is not one of them.

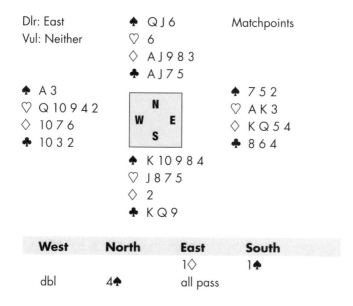

Dlr: East
Vul: Neither

♠ Q J 6
♡ 6
◇ A J 9 8 3
♣ A J 7 5

Matchpoints

♠ A 3
♡ Q 10 9 4 2
◇ 10 7 6
♣ 10 3 2

♠ 7 5 2
♡ A K 3
◇ K Q 5 4
♣ 8 6 4

♠ K 10 9 8 4
♡ J 8 7 5
◇ 2
♣ K Q 9

West	North	East	South
		1◇	1♠
dbl	4♠	all pass	

How will you play the spade game when West makes the bright start of the ace of trumps followed by another trump? Without this awkward lead, you would have been able to score a heart ruff to bring your total to ten tricks. How can you recover the lost ground?

You unblock dummy's ♣J on the first trick and win the trump continuation in your hand. Four trumps, four clubs and the ◇A add up to only nine. You will have to establish an extra diamond trick to make the game. At Trick 3 you lead a low diamond and play the ◇8 from dummy, hoping that West holds the ◇10. Your luck is in when East wins with the ◇Q.

When a third round of trumps is returned, you win in the dummy and play the ◇A, throwing a heart. You continue with the ◇J, covered by the ◇K and ruffed, and West's ◇10 is pinned. It is then a simple matter to play four rounds of clubs and the two established diamonds, discarding all three remaining hearts for an amazing overtrick.

(This deal might have been included in the section on matchpoint defense. If East wanted to score a heart trick, he needed to take it at Trick 3, before removing dummy's last trump!)

Recovering when you are in an inferior contract

Dummy goes down and you see that you are not in the best matchpoint contract. We all know that feeling! Rather than resign yourself to a low score, look for an opportunity to rescue the situation.

```
Dlr: South          ♠ 6 4              Matchpoints
Vul: E-W            ♡ Q 7 3
                    ◇ Q 10 9
                    ♣ J 10 8 6 5

♠ Q J 10 9 3              N          ♠ A 7 5 2
♡ 9 2                              ♡ 6 4
◇ 7 4 2         W         E        ◇ K 8 5 3
♣ 9 4 3                  S          ♣ K Q 7

                    ♠ K 8
                    ♡ A K J 10 8 5
                    ◇ A J 6
                    ♣ A 2
```

West	North	East	South
			2♣
pass	2◇	pass	2NT
pass	3NT	all pass	

You decide against a 1♡ opening and are unwilling to commit to a game-forcing 2♣-2◇-2♡ sequence. Rightly or wrongly, you decide to open 2♣ and rebid 2NT. Partner raises to 3NT and West leads the ♠Q to East's ♠A. Back comes another spade to your king and you pause to assess the situation.

One spade, six hearts, one diamond and one club will give you +400 for nine tricks. That is how you would play the contract at IMPs. In a matchpoint game nearly all the other tables will be playing in 4♡, scoring +420 or +450, depending on whether the diamond finesse succeeds. It would be giving up to cash your top nine tricks. Even though the spades are bare and a losing diamond finesse will cost the contract, you must steel yourself to take that finesse!

When the cards lie as in the diagram, the finesse will win and you will score +460 for a top. What if the diamond finesse had failed? You would have gone one down, picking up −50. This would be very little worse (if at all) than +400. So, you have little to lose by taking the diamond finesse — and almost a whole top to gain.

Recovering from a bad break

Sometimes you bid to a good contract (yes, it can happen...) and suffer a bad break early in the play. At matchpoints, this will happen to other declarers too. You must think hard; what is the best remaining chance of landing the contract? Test yourself on this deal:

Dlr: South
Vul: E-W

Matchpoints

	North	
	♠ 10 9 7 6 2	
	♡ J	
	◇ K J 10 7	
	♣ 10 9 4	

West		East
♠ J 8 4 3		♠ —
♡ 10 9 8 5	N	♡ 7 6 4 3 2
◇ 6 4 2	W E	◇ 9 8 5 3
♣ 8 3	S	♣ K 7 6 2

	South	
	♠ A K Q 5	
	♡ A K Q	
	◇ A Q	
	♣ A Q J 5	

West	North	East	South
			2♣
pass	2◇	pass	6NT
pass	7NT	all pass	

Whatever the opponents think of the bidding, you cannot be accused of wasting anyone's time with a tortuous bidding sequence. West leads the ♡10 against 7NT and you see that five spades, three hearts, four diamonds and the ♣A add up to (hurray!) thirteen.

You win with the ♡A, play the ♠A and... East discards a heart. What sort of reward is that for reaching such an excellent matchpoint contract? How will you continue?

With only three spade tricks available, you will need to score three club tricks (taking a finesse that would have been an unnecessary risk in 6NT). You play the ◇A and overtake the ◇Q with the ◇K. You cash the ◇J, throwing the ♠5 from your hand. What should you discard on the ◇10?

If you mistakenly throw the ♣5, you would have to win the first round of clubs in the South hand with the ♣J or ♣Q. You would not then be able to repeat the club finesse. Instead, you must throw the ♣J (or ♣Q). You can then lead the ♣10, following with the ♣5 when East doesn't cover. The finesse wins and you can then take a second club finesse to rescue the contract. You make 7NT and justice is done.

Foreseeing a bad break

It is one thing to recover from a bad break that is already apparent. Sometimes you must foresee a bad break before it happens and play accordingly. What would you have made of this contract?

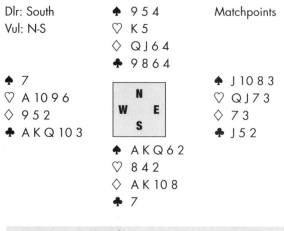

Dlr: South	♠ 9 5 4	Matchpoints
Vul: N-S	♡ K 5	
	◇ Q J 6 4	
	♣ 9 8 6 4	

West:
♠ 7
♡ A 10 9 6
◇ 9 5 2
♣ A K Q 10 3

East:
♠ J 10 8 3
♡ Q J 7 3
◇ 7 3
♣ J 5 2

South:
♠ A K Q 6 2
♡ 8 4 2
◇ A K 10 8
♣ 7

West	North	East	South
			1♠
dbl	2♠	pass	4♠
all pass			

West leads the ♣K, which asks for a count signal in his methods. (The ♣A would have asked for an attitude signal.) East follows with the ♣2, proclaiming an odd number of clubs. You ruff the ♣A continuation and play a heart to the king, which wins. East wins the second round of hearts and returns the ♣J, which you ruff. You ruff a heart in dummy and return to your hand with the ♠A, all following. What now?

If trumps break 3-2, you can simply draw trumps and score five trumps, four diamonds, the ♡K and a heart ruff. That will make a very satisfactory +650. What is the chance of a 3-2 trump break, would you say? The reference books will tell you that it's around 68%. Yes, but that is in the absence of other distributional information. The early fall of the cards suggests that West holds ♣AKQ103. Since he doubled rather than overcalling 2♣ (and probably did not play the ♡A on the first three rounds), you can also place him with four hearts. He would hardly have doubled on 3=4=1=5 shape, so you can immediately discard the half of the 68% where West would hold three spades. Some players would not double on 2=4=2=5 shape either. In other words, the odds are strongly in favor of a 4-1 trump break. How should you continue the play?

You should abandon the trump suit for the moment, leaving the ♠9 in dummy and the ♠KQ in your hand (East has ♠J108). You play three rounds of diamonds and East has no answer. He has to ruff or you would have ten tricks. If he then plays a fourth round of hearts, you can ruff with dummy's ♠9 for your tenth trick; if instead he returns a trump, you will draw trumps and score the fourth diamond. Brilliant! Any pairs who do not analyze as you have done, playing for a 3-2 break in trumps, will go down.

SUMMARY

- When you end in the second-best matchpoint contract or a defender makes an unusual but successful opening lead against you, look for some way to rescue your score.

- One possibility is to take a finesse that you would not otherwise risk. If the finesse happens to fail, it will cost you very little. You will get much the same score for making two tricks fewer than the field as you would if you settled for one trick fewer.

- Another possibility of regaining a trick is to play one of the suits in a slightly anti-percentage way. For example, you might play to drop a missing honor when you expect the other declarers to take a finesse.

- Don't be dispirited when you suffer a bad break in a suit — one that may well defeat the contract. Other declarers will be in the same position. Maybe there is a way to rescue the situation by finding a favorable lie in some other suit. If not, you must still concentrate on restricting the damage to just one down.

Test Yourself

1.   Dlr: South   ♠ A 6   Matchpoints
       Vul: Neither   ♡ K 8 7 4
                       ◇ 10 8 7 2
                       ♣ A 4 2

                       ♠ 5 3
                       ♡ A Q J 10 5
                       ◇ A Q
                       ♣ K Q J 10

West	North	East	South
			1♡
pass	3♡	4♠	5♣
pass	6♡	all pass	

You win West's ♠2 lead with dummy's ♠A and play a trump, East discarding a spade. How will you play the slam?

2.   Dlr: South   ♠ A J 10 8 2   Matchpoints
       Vul: Both   ♡ A 9
                       ◇ 8 6 5
                       ♣ K 8 3

                       ♠ K 9 7
                       ♡ 10 6 5 2
                       ◇ A K 7 4
                       ♣ A 4

West	North	East	South
			1◇
pass	1♠	pass	1NT
pass	3NT	all pass	

How will you play 3NT when West leads the ♣Q?

ANSWERS

1.

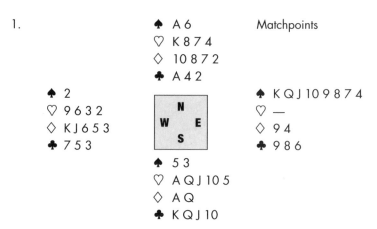

	♠ A 6	Matchpoints
	♡ K 8 7 4	
	◇ 10 8 7 2	
	♣ A 4 2	

♠ 2   ♠ K Q J 10 9 8 7 4
♡ 9 6 3 2   ♡ —
◇ K J 6 5 3   ◇ 9 4
♣ 7 5 3   ♣ 9 8 6

♠ 5 3
♡ A Q J 10 5
◇ A Q
♣ K Q J 10

West leads the ♠2 against 6♡. Unless trumps are 4-0, you can draw trumps and discard a spade from dummy on the fourth club. A spade ruff will then give you a twelfth trick. When you play a trump, East shows out. You should draw three rounds of trumps and then play four clubs, throwing the dummy's ♣6. If West ruffs the second or third club, he will have to return a diamond into your ◇AQ.

2.

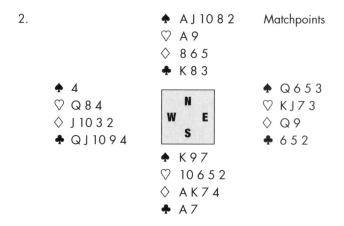

	♠ A J 10 8 2	Matchpoints
	♡ A 9	
	◇ 8 6 5	
	♣ K 8 3	

♠ 4   ♠ Q 6 5 3
♡ Q 8 4   ♡ K J 7 3
◇ J 10 3 2   ◇ Q 9
♣ Q J 10 9 4   ♣ 6 5 2

♠ K 9 7
♡ 10 6 5 2
◇ A K 7 4
♣ A 7

West leads the ♣Q against 3NT. Many Norths will use check-back, ending in 4♠. They will ruff a club in the South hand, continuing with the ♠K and a finesse of the ♠J. If this line picks up the trump suit, they will score eleven tricks for +650. The best chance of beating them is to finesse spades the other way. Win with the ♣K and run the ♠J. When East holds the ♠Q, you will score +630 against their +620. (If your spade finesse wins, duck a diamond and seek an extra diamond trick for +660.)

14

LOOKING FOR OVERTRICKS

How much is an overtrick worth? When playing IMPs, it will give you an extra 20 or 30, probably worth 1 IMP. At matchpoints, that small extra amount may be worth half a top! Look at this deal:

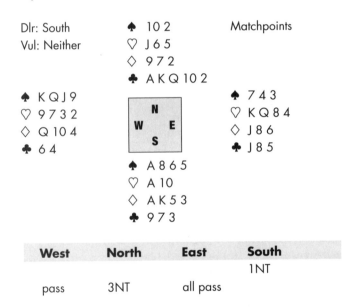

Dlr: South
Vul: Neither

Matchpoints

North hand:
♠ 10 2
♡ J 6 5
◇ 9 7 2
♣ A K Q 10 2

West hand:
♠ K Q J 9
♡ 9 7 3 2
◇ Q 10 4
♣ 6 4

East hand:
♠ 7 4 3
♡ K Q 8 4
◇ J 8 6
♣ J 8 5

South hand:
♠ A 8 6 5
♡ A 10
◇ A K 5 3
♣ 9 7 3

West	North	East	South
			1NT
pass	3NT	all pass	

North quite rightly heads straight for 3NT. It is pointless to introduce the club suit on such a moderate hand, since nine tricks in 3NT are much more likely than eleven in clubs. At matchpoints, there is a further consideration. If declarer can make ten tricks in 3NT, this will outscore even twelve tricks in 5♣. How will you play the notrump game when West leads the ♠K?

Since you are not afraid of any switch, you should hold up the ♠A until the third round. East follows three times, so West has only one spade winner left. You continue with the ace and king of clubs, pleased to see both defenders follow suit. Nine tricks are now guaranteed. Are you happy with that or will you look for an overtrick?

At matchpoints, it is vital to look for +430 instead of +400. What chances can you see of a tenth trick? Look at the diamond suit. If it breaks 3-3 (a 36% chance) you can set up an extra trick there. However, you will have to give up a round of diamonds, and West may well win this and cash his spade winner. (Even if West holds ◊Jxx, his partner will have the chance to ditch the ◊Q under your ◊AK. He will place West with the ◊J since you did not take a finesse in the suit.)

A better chance is to find East with the ♡K and ♡Q. After just two rounds of clubs you lead a heart, planning to finesse the ♡10. If East does hold both the missing heart honors, it will make no difference if he splits them on the first round. You will win and knock out his remaining honor. Suppose your finesse of the ♡10 loses to West. Nothing has been lost! He cashes a spade, yes, but you will still score +400.

When the cards lie as in the diagram, this may be the matchpoint table:

N-S	E-W	Contract	By	Tricks	N-S score	E-W score	N-S MPs	E-W MPs
1	5	3NT	S	9	400		3	4
2	4	3NT	S	10	430		6.5	0.5
3	7	5♣	N	10		50	0	7
4	1	3NT	S	9	400		3	4
5	6	3NT	S	9	400		3	4
6	3	5♣	N	11	400		3	4
7	8	3NT	N	9	400		3	4
8	2	3NT	S	10	430		6.5	0.5

Sitting N-S Pair 2, you score a joint top with 6.5 MPs out of 7 for your overtrick in 3NT. As often happens, the overtrick is worth half a top; you gain 3.5 matchpoints.

Two pairs alighted in the inferior contract of 5♣, one of them escaping a spade lead and rescuing a reasonable board by discarding a spade on the thirteenth diamond.

Everyone knows that +430 will score more matchpoints than +400. On the deal that we have just seen, you could go for the overtrick without risking the contract. The question arises: when should you risk your contract in the search for a valuable overtrick?

Let's take a close look at this 3NT contract:

Dlr: North
Vul: N-S

	♠ 5 2	Matchpoints
	♡ A Q 6	
	◇ A Q J 10 9 5	
	♣ A 7	

♠ 10 9 8 3
♡ J 9 4
◇ 8 6
♣ K 10 9 4

```
      N
  W       E
      S
```

♠ K Q J 7 6
♡ K 8 5
◇ 7 3
♣ Q 6 5

♠ A 4
♡ 10 7 3 2
◇ K 4 2
♣ J 8 3 2

West	**North**	**East**	**South**
	1◇	1♠	dbl
2♠	3◇	pass	3NT
all pass			

You start with a negative double and then try your luck in 3NT, expecting to make several diamond tricks. How should you play the contract when West leads the ♠10, East following with the ♠7?

You have nine tricks on top, so the contract is guaranteed. Should you finesse the ♡Q, seeking to turn +600 into +630?

The first question to ask is: are you in the normal contract? You have a combined total of 25 HCPs and a powerful six-card diamond suit. You can expect most pairs to find the good 3NT contract, but a few may stop in a diamond partscore. It's not possible to estimate precisely, but +600 may give you a 60% score. Suppose you take a heart finesse and it wins. +630 may then give you a 90% score. If the finesse loses and you go minus, your score will be very poor, perhaps 10%. If we assume for the moment that the heart finesse has a 50% chance of winning, you will have an expectation of 50% (half of 90% + half of 10%) if you take the finesse. This is less than the 60% you expect from taking your nine top tricks.

Next you must ask yourself: what is the chance that the heart finesse will succeed? West has shown some values with his raise. He may hold the ♡K, he may not. If East holds ♠KQJxx, the heart finesse may well be close to a 50% chance, as we assumed above.

Well, there you have it. It's a rough calculation, but it seems that you will lose out in the long run by taking the heart finesse. *You will be risking a near bottom.* The general idea, when playing pairs, is to collect a few tops, either by your superior play or by the opponents' mistakes. On the rest of the boards, you aim to collect average scores or maybe just above average. In that way you can amass a total above 60%, you hope, giving you a chance to win the event.

Sometimes you can judge that an all-or-nothing finesse has more than a 50% chance:

Dlr: West	♠ 10 2	Matchpoints
Vul: N-S	♡ 9 7 3 2	
	◇ A K 6 5	
	♣ Q J 4	

♠ K Q J 9 5 3		♠ 7 6
♡ J 8	**N**	♡ K 10 6 4
◇ 9 4 3	**W** **E**	◇ Q J 8 2
♣ 10 5	**S**	♣ 8 6 3

	♠ A 8 4
	♡ A Q 5
	◇ 10 7
	♣ A K 9 7 2

West	North	East	South
2♠	pass	pass	2NT
pass	3NT	all pass	

West, who opened a weak 2♠, leads the ♠K against 3NT. You have nine top tricks, so the contract is secure. Immediately, your mind turns towards a possible overtrick. How will you play?

If East holds the ♡K, a successful finesse of the ♡Q will give you the overtrick that you seek. How likely is it that the finesse will win? West's magnificent spades are sufficient to justify a 2♠ opening. He might hold the ♡K; he might not. There are two slight indications that make East the favorite to hold the ♡K. The first is that if West holds that card, the addition of a diamond honor would make him rather strong for a 2♠ opening, and he might choose to open 1♠ instead. The second is that East holds eleven non-spades to West's seven. That makes him an initial 11:7 favorite to hold any missing cards outside spades.

Since you are not worried about a switch elsewhere, you hold up the ♠A until the third round. When you continue with five club tricks, West follows twice and then discards two diamonds and a spade. You cross to the ◇K, West following with his last diamond. You have reached the crossroads. Should you finesse the ♡Q or play to the ♡A, settling for nine tricks?

Before deciding, you should cash the other top diamond, reducing West to three cards. If he discards another spade, his remaining cards will be one spade and two hearts. It is safe then to take the heart finesse!

Suppose he discards a heart instead, keeping two spades and one heart. What now?

At IMPs, you would not think of risking the contract (if West was down to two spade winners and the bare ♡K). You would be endangering your certain +600 in the search for an extra +30. At matchpoints, you should finesse! West's shape appears to be 6=2=3=2. East began with four hearts to West's two and is therefore a 2:1 favorite to hold the ♡K. By finessing, you will gain around half a top two times in every three and lose half a top one time in three. Play safe, rising with the ♡A and the opposite is the case; you will lose half a top two times in three. Your odds are improved by the fact that many defenders would not dare to bare the ♡K, in case you play to the ♡A and score an overtrick that way.

We will end the chapter with a deal where many players would not even realize that there was a chance of scoring an overtrick:

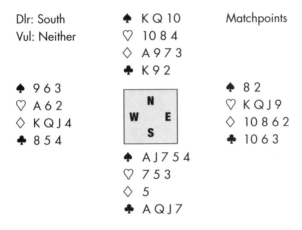

Dlr: South	♠ K Q 10	Matchpoints
Vul: Neither	♡ 10 8 4	
	◇ A 9 7 3	
	♣ K 9 2	

```
♠ 9 6 3              ♠ 8 2
♡ A 6 2         N    ♡ K Q J 9
◇ K Q J 4    W   E   ◇ 10 8 6 2
♣ 8 5 4         S    ♣ 10 6 3
```

```
             ♠ A J 7 5 4
             ♡ 7 5 3
             ◇ 5
             ♣ A Q J 7
```

West	North	East	South
			1♠
pass	2◇	pass	2♠
pass	4♠	all pass	

You reach 4♠ at matchpoints. How will you play this contract when West leads the ◇K?

'Dull hand,' some players would say. 'Five spades, four clubs and the ◇A for a total of ten. Nothing more to it!'

That's not quite right. If trumps break 3-2, you can play on dummy reversal lines, ruffing three diamonds in the South hand. Three trump tricks in dummy and three ruffs in your hand, along with five minor-suit winners will bring your total to eleven tricks.

After winning the diamond lead, you ruff a diamond in your hand. You cross to the ♠10 and ruff another diamond with the ♠J. You return to dummy with a second round of trumps (pleased to see both defenders follow) and ruff the last diamond with the ♠A. Finally, you lead to the ♣K and draw the last trump. Three more rounds of clubs will bring your total to eleven.

Playing for an overtrick in this fashion may see you go down when trumps do not break 3-2. You would therefore not risk such a line of play at IMPs. Since a 3-2 break occurs 68% of the time, you should go boldly for the overtrick at matchpoints. You will score a shared top with eleven tricks 68% of the time. Otherwise, you will score nine or ten tricks, depending on the club break.

SUMMARY

- When most of the matchpoint field is likely to be in the same contract, an overtrick can be worth half a top.

- You are entitled to risk your contract seeking such an overtrick when the chance of success is appreciably better than 50%. (It makes no real difference to the situation whether you judge that most of the field will take this risk or not.)

- For example, if your attempt at an overtrick will succeed when trumps break 3-2 (a 68% chance) and you will go down in the contract when trumps break less well (a 32% chance), you should go ahead and try for the overtrick.

- When instead you are in a good contract that may not be widely bid, you should generally refuse to put the contract at risk by seeking an overtrick (see Chapter 16 — Playing a Good Contract).

Teſt Yourſelf

1.

♠ 8 6 4
♡ 10 8 7 6
♢ 9 7 5 3
♣ K 6

Matchpoints

♠ A K
♡ A 5
♢ A K 2
♣ A Q J 10 5 4

West	North	East	South
			2♣
pass	2♢	pass	3♣
pass	3♢	pass	3NT
all pass			

West leads the ♠Q against 3NT. How will you play?

2.

♠ 8 6 5 2
♡ A K 7
♢ 9 8 3
♣ A 10 2

Matchpoints

♠ A K Q J 9
♡ 10 5 4 2
♢ A K 7
♣ 9

West	North	East	South
			1♠
pass	3♠	pass	4♠
all pass			

West leads the ♡6 against your contract of 4♠. You win with dummy's ♡A and play a trump to the ♠A, East discarding the ♣3. How will you continue?

3.   ♠ K 6   Matchpoints
                                 ♡ Q 6 2
                                 ♢ A 9 4
                                 ♣ K Q 9 8 6
                                 ▭
                                 ♠ A Q 5
                                 ♡ K 10 5 4
                                 ♢ Q 6 2
                                 ♣ J 10 4

West	North	East	South
1♢	2♣	pass	2NT
pass	3NT	all pass	

West leads the ♠3 against 3NT. You win with the ♠K and play the ♣K to West's ♣A. He persists with spades and later turns up with three clubs. How will you look for an overtrick or two?

4.   ♠ Q 10 8 2   Matchpoints
                                 ♡ A J
                                 ♢ A 7 3
                                 ♣ K Q 6 3
                                 ▭
                                 ♠ A K J 9 6 3
                                 ♡ 7 4 3
                                 ♢ 10 8 6
                                 ♣ 2

West	North	East	South
			2♠
pass	4♠	all pass	

West leads the ♣J against your contract of 4♠. After this helpful lead, ten tricks will be easy. Is there any chance of an overtrick?

ANSWERS

1.

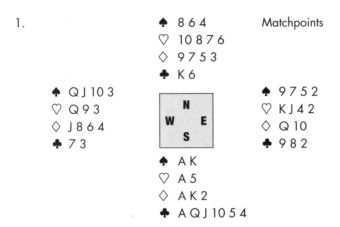

West leads the ♠Q against 3NT and you win with the ♠A. The contract is secure, so you must look for overtricks. You have eleven top tricks. The main chance of a twelfth trick is to find the diamonds breaking 3-3. In some situations you might lead the ◇2 from your hand, intending to play the ◇AK before crossing to dummy on the second round of clubs. Here it is slightly better to play ace, king and another diamond, since this will also generate a twelfth trick when East began with ◇QJ, ◇Q10 or ◇J10.

2.

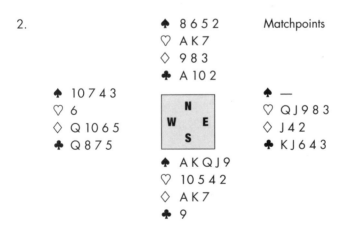

West leads the ♡6 against 4♠. You win with the ♡A and play a trump to the ♠A, East throwing a club. Seeking an overtrick, you lead a heart towards dummy. If West ruffs a loser, you can draw trumps and ruff your last heart. If instead he discards, you win with the ♡K and give up a heart. You win the diamond return, play the ♠KQ and lead your last heart. If West ruffs with the ♠10, you will discard a diamond from dummy and ruff a diamond for your overtrick

3.

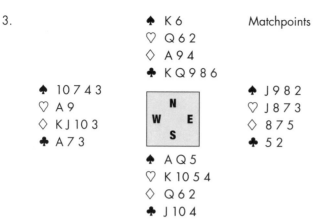

                        ♠ K 6   Matchpoints
                        ♡ Q 6 2
                        ◇ A 9 4
                        ♣ K Q 9 8 6

♠ 10 7 4 3   ♠ J 9 8 2
♡ A 9   ♡ J 8 7 3
◇ K J 10 3   ◇ 8 7 5
♣ A 7 3   ♣ 5 2

                        ♠ A Q 5
                        ♡ K 10 5 4
                        ◇ Q 6 2
                        ♣ J 10 4

West, who opened 1◇, leads the ♠3 against 3NT. You win with the ♠K
and play the ♣K. West wins with the ♣A and persists with another
spade to your queen. You play the ♣J10 and West follows all the way.
You lead a low heart and West plays the ♡9, dummy's ♡Q winning. If
West holds four spades, which is likely, his shape will be 4=2=4=3. On
the next round of hearts, East plays the ♡7 and you should play the ♡5!
West's ♡A appears and you can later finesse the ♡10 to give you +660
and a matchpoint top.

4.

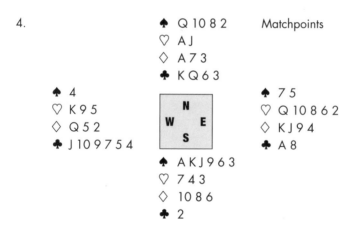

                        ♠ Q 10 8 2   Matchpoints
                        ♡ A J
                        ◇ A 7 3
                        ♣ K Q 6 3

♠ 4   ♠ 7 5
♡ K 9 5   ♡ Q 10 8 6 2
◇ Q 5 2   ◇ K J 9 4
♣ J 10 9 7 5 4   ♣ A 8

                        ♠ A K J 9 6 3
                        ♡ 7 4 3
                        ◇ 10 8 6
                        ♣ 2

West leads the ♣J against 4♠. After this helpful lead, you can discard
one of your diamond losers on a club honor, which will secure the contract. Is there any chance of an overtrick? Yes! You should play low from
dummy on the first trick, hoping that East began with ♣Ax. Let's say
that West switches to a low diamond. You win with the ◇A and draw
trumps with the ♠A and ♠10. When you lead dummy's remaining low
club, the ♣A appears from East! You can then discard both diamond
losers on the ♣KQ and make an overtrick. If the ♣A didn't fall in two
rounds, you would take a ruffing finesse in clubs to make the contract.

15

Playing in a Sacrifice

In this chapter we see how you should tackle a sacrifice contract. You must set yourself a target penalty and arrange the play with this in mind. In a matchpoint event, the target that you set may depend on what you think will happen at other tables. Take the South cards here:

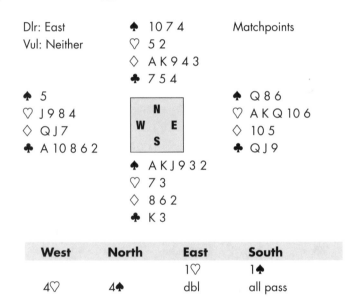

Dlr: East
Vul: Neither

Matchpoints

North
♠ 10 7 4
♡ 5 2
♢ A K 9 4 3
♣ 7 5 4

West
♠ 5
♡ J 9 8 4
♢ Q J 7
♣ A 10 8 6 2

East
♠ Q 8 6
♡ A K Q 10 6
♢ 10 5
♣ Q J 9

South
♠ A K J 9 3 2
♡ 7 3
♢ 8 6 2
♣ K 3

West	North	East	South
		1♡	1♠
4♡	4♠	dbl	all pass

West leads the ♡4 against your 4♠ sacrifice. East wins with the ♡Q, cashes the ♡A and switches to the ♣Q. Without much hope, you cover with the ♣K. West wins with the ♣A and returns a club to his partner's ♣J. How will you continue the play when East returns with a third round of clubs?

You have lost four tricks already and an eventual diamond loser will make that five. You must now judge how to play the trump suit. When you play the ♠A, both defenders

THINK ABOUT...

Suppose you sacrifice in 4♠ and go 300 down. If you subsequently discover that the opponents would not have made their 4♡ contract, you have made what is called a **phantom sacrifice.**

follow with low spot cards. Will you play for the drop now or cross to dummy to finesse against the ♠Q?

There are two good reasons why you should finesse against the ♠Q on the second round. Firstly, if trumps are 2-2, it is likely that you could have beaten 4♡ with two spade tricks and two diamond tricks. Losing 300 may be a poor score anyway, in that case. Secondly, West's leap to 4♡ on a weakish hand suggests that he will hold a singleton spade.

You cross to the ◊A and finesse the ♠J. Hurray, West shows out! You have restricted the penalty to 300 and — more importantly — all the pairs allowed to play in 4♡ will collect 420. It will be a good board for you.

Sometimes the prevailing vulnerability affects how you play a sacrifice.

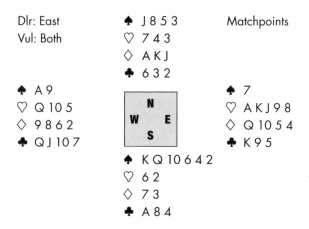

Dlr: East	♠ J 8 5 3	Matchpoints
Vul: Both	♡ 7 4 3	
	◊ A K J	
	♣ 6 3 2	

West hand:
♠ A 9
♡ Q 10 5
◊ 9 8 6 2
♣ Q J 10 7

East hand:
♠ 7
♡ A K J 9 8
◊ Q 10 5 4
♣ K 9 5

South hand:
♠ K Q 10 6 4 2
♡ 6 2
◊ 7 3
♣ A 8 4

West	North	East	South
		1♡	2♠
3♡	4♠	dbl	all pass

How will you play 4♠ doubled when West leads the ♣Q?

If you win the first or second round of clubs and play a trump, the defenders will score five tricks for a 500 penalty. The question is: should you finesse the ◊J before playing on trumps, hoping to set up a discard for one of your losers?

With both sides vulnerable, the answer is 'No!' Regardless of the fate of 4♡ elsewhere, it will make no difference to those comparisons whether you lose 200 or 500. What will make a difference is if you take an unsuccessful diamond finesse and go down 800, losing more than the value of the opponents' 4♡.

Suppose that (perhaps unwisely) you had sacrificed in 4♠ when vulnerable against non-vulnerable. Going 500 down against a potential

420 the other way would be an awful board. You would have to take the diamond finesse, hoping to escape for a 200 penalty and beat the pairs making 420 in the heart game.

Right, test yourself on this one:

```
Dlr: East          ♠ K 7 5          Matchpoints
Vul: Neither       ♡ 4
                   ◇ 8 6 4 2
                   ♣ J 10 9 4 2

♠ 10 3                              ♠ 9 6 2
♡ Q 7 5 2           N              ♡ A K J 10 3
◇ K 9 5 3       W       E          ◇ J 10 7
♣ K Q 7             S              ♣ A 6

                   ♠ A Q J 8 4
                   ♡ 9 8 6
                   ◇ A Q
                   ♣ 8 5 3
```

West	North	East	South
		1♡	1♠
2♠	3♠	4♡	4♠
dbl	all pass		

East wins the heart lead and switches to a trump. How will you play?

You win with the ♠J and ruff one of your heart losers. You must now decide whether to finesse the ◇Q. If the finesse loses, the defenders will remove dummy's last trump and you will go three down for –500. If instead the finesse wins, you will escape for –100. If 4♡ was failing, any minus score may be bad. When 4♡ is worth 420 for E-W, you should be happy to lose only 300. So, cross to your ◇A and take the second heart ruff.

SUMMARY

- Sometimes your play in a sacrifice is affected by the fact that a particular lie of the cards would beat the opponents' contract. Since a 'phantom sacrifice' is likely to score badly, you should assume a different lie.

- When it is likely that the opponents would have made their game, you must strive to reduce the penalty to less than the value of their game. Do this, even if you risk going an extra one down.

- When you hold such a big fit that it seems the matchpoint field may be taking the same sacrifice as you, plan your play to compete with them, rather than with those who choose to defend the opponents' game.

Te/t Your/elf

1. Dlr: West   ♠ Q 10 5   Matchpoints
    Vul: Neither   ♡ 10 6
                    ◇ A 4 3 2
                    ♣ A 8 3 2

                    ♠ A K J 4 3
                    ♡ 4 2
                    ◇ 9 8 5
                    ♣ 7 5 4

West	North	East	South
1♡	pass	2♡	2♠
4♡	4♠	dbl	all pass

West leads the ♡Q and continues with the ♡J, overtaken with the ♡K. East switches to the ♣Q. How will you play the contract?

2. Dlr: East   ♠ K 2   Matchpoints
    Vul: Neither   ♡ 8 5 3
                    ◇ Q J 5 4
                    ♣ Q 10 6 3

                    ♠ A J 9 8 5 4
                    ♡ Q
                    ◇ K 9 6 3
                    ♣ J 7

West	North	East	South
		3♡	3♠
4♡	4♠	pass	pass
dbl	all pass		

You wouldn't have bid 4♠ on that North hand perhaps. Well, it's done now. How will you play 4♠ doubled when West leads the ♣K (East playing the ♣2 to show an odd number of clubs) and West switches to king and another heart?

1.

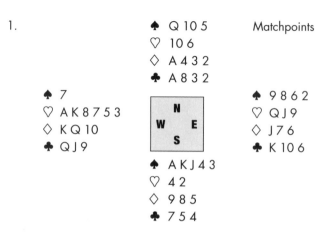

♠ Q 10 5
♡ 10 6
◇ A 4 3 2
♣ A 8 3 2

Matchpoints

♠ 7
♡ A K 8 7 5 3
◇ K Q 10
♣ Q J 9

♠ 9 8 6 2
♡ Q J 9
◇ J 7 6
♣ K 10 6

♠ A K J 4 3
♡ 4 2
◇ 9 8 5
♣ 7 5 4

If spades are 4-1, E-W's 4♡ would have been successful. Going two down for 300 will be a good sacrifice. West scores two hearts and switches to the ♣Q, which you duck. If West now plays the ◇K, you must duck that too. Say that West next plays the ♣J. You win with the ♣A, draw trumps and give up a club. When clubs break 3-3, you can discard a diamond and escape for −300. If instead you win the first round of one minor suit, the opponents will have time to clear their tricks in the other minor.

2.

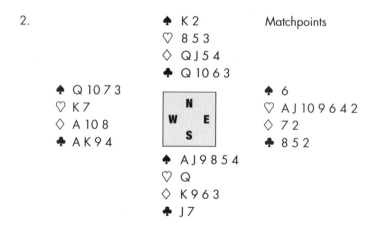

♠ K 2
♡ 8 5 3
◇ Q J 5 4
♣ Q 10 6 3

Matchpoints

♠ Q 10 7 3
♡ K 7
◇ A 10 8
♣ A K 9 4

♠ 6
♡ A J 10 9 6 4 2
◇ 7 2
♣ 8 5 2

♠ A J 9 8 5 4
♡ Q
◇ K 9 6 3
♣ J 7

West leads the ♣K against 4♠ doubled. East signals an odd number and West switches to king and another heart. You ruff the second round and see that you must lose only one trump to escape for two down. (Minus 500 would be more than their heart game). After his preempt, East is a big favorite to hold a singleton trump, particularly as he seems to have three cards in clubs. At Trick 4, you should lead the ♠J, planning to run it. When East holds a singleton 10, 7, 6 or 3, you will lose only one trump.

16

Playing a Good Contract

Suppose you are playing matchpoints and reach a high-scoring contract, one that you suspect other pairs may not reach. You are entitled to play the contract safely to protect your good score. Look at this deal:

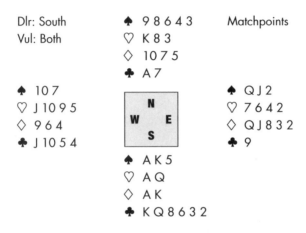

Dlr: South
Vul: Both

North
♠ 9 8 6 4 3
♡ K 8 3
◇ 10 7 5
♣ A 7

West
♠ 10 7
♡ J 10 9 5
◇ 9 6 4
♣ J 10 5 4

East
♠ Q J 2
♡ 7 6 4 2
◇ Q J 8 3 2
♣ 9

South
♠ A K 5
♡ A Q
◇ A K
♣ K Q 8 6 3 2

Matchpoints

West	North	East	South
			2♣
pass	2◇	pass	3NT
pass	6NT	all pass	

Your partner judges that 6NT will score more highly than a possible 6♠. How will you play the notrump slam when West leads the ♡J?

If clubs break 3-2, which is a 68% chance, you will have thirteen top tricks to take. Suppose you play in straightforward fashion, scoring the two top hearts in your hand and crossing to the ♣A to make the ♡K. When you return to hand with the ♣K, East will show out. You will need to surrender a club trick to set up the suit, and West will then cash a heart for one down. Unlucky, yes, but what could you have done about it?

At IMPs you would have played the hand more safely. After taking the two heart winners in your hand, you would duck a round of clubs. On any return you would then be able to use the ♣A to reach the third heart winner. Twelve tricks would be yours. In short, you would duck a round of clubs when it was safe to do so (while you still held a heart stopper).

The question is: should you play this way at matchpoints — surrendering a 68% chance of +1470 and a top score? You should, because you expect +1440 to be a good score anyway, even if the clubs break 3-2. Those pairs who locate the spade fit and play in 6♠ cannot score more than +1430. Any pair in 6♣ will not come close to your +1440. Finally, there will be some pairs that stop in game.

So, do not be too greedy when you reach a good contract. If you judge that you will get a 70-80% score by playing safely and foregoing a possible overtrick, this is what you should do.

South judged that he had reached a good contract on this deal too:

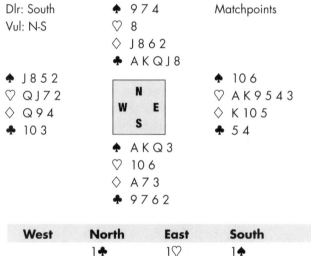

Dlr: South	♠ 9 7 4	Matchpoints
Vul: N-S	♡ 8	
	◇ J 8 6 2	
	♣ A K Q J 8	

West
♠ J 8 5 2
♡ Q J 7 2
◇ Q 9 4
♣ 10 3

East
♠ 10 6
♡ A K 9 5 4 3
◇ K 10 5
♣ 5 4

South
♠ A K Q 3
♡ 10 6
◇ A 7 3
♣ 9 7 6 2

West	North	East	South
	1♣	1♡	1♠
2♡	2♠	pass	4♠
all pass			

West led the ♡Q against the spade game and continued with the ♡2, ruffed in the dummy. How would you play the contract at matchpoints?

If trumps break 3-3, you can draw trumps and claim eleven top tricks. Suppose that East shows out on the third round of trumps. You cannot rescue the situation by turning to the clubs, aiming to lose one heart, one trump (when West ruffs a club) and one diamond — throwing the other diamond loser on the fifth round of clubs. West will delay his club ruff until the fourth round! You will then lose two diamond tricks and go one down.

Making ten tricks for +620 will surely be a good score on this deal, even if trumps do break 3-3. You should therefore aim to preserve the advantage that you have won by reaching such an excellent contract. Do you see how you can guard against a 4-2 trump break?

After ruffing a heart at Trick 2, you must duck a round of trumps. You lose a trump trick at a moment when the defenders can do you no damage. Dummy will still have a trump to protect you against a third round of hearts. On any return, you will be able to draw trumps and claim ten tricks (three trumps, one heart ruff, the ◇A and five club tricks).

Counting the hand to choose the best line

Suppose you reach a contract that will depend on locating a missing queen. It is a familiar technique to play the other three suits first, seeking a partial or complete count on the deal. The defender who holds the greater length in the key suit is then more likely to hold the missing queen.

Counting the hand can help you to calculate the best line of play in other circumstances, too. Test yourself on this slam:

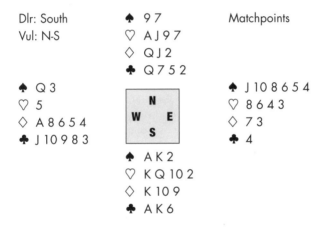

Dlr: South
Vul: N-S

♠ 9 7
♡ A J 9 7
◇ Q J 2
♣ Q 7 5 2

Matchpoints

♠ Q 3
♡ 5
◇ A 8 6 5 4
♣ J 10 9 8 3

♠ J 10 8 6 5 4
♡ 8 6 4 3
◇ 7 3
♣ 4

♠ A K 2
♡ K Q 10 2
◇ K 10 9
♣ A K 6

West	North	East	South
			2♣
pass	2◇	pass	2NT
pass	3♣	pass	3♡
pass	6♡	all pass	

At matchpoints, your partner had to choose between 6♡ and 6NT. Since the combined point count was not especially high for a small slam (around 32-33), he opted for the 4-4 heart fit. Has he made the right decision?

It looks like it! You will have eleven tricks once you have set up the diamonds. A twelfth trick should be easy in 6♡ because you can ruff a spade in dummy. In the inferior contract of 6NT you would need a 3-3 club break.

West leads the ♣J against your heart slam and you win with the ♣A. When you play the ace and king of trumps, bad news arrives — West shows out, throwing a diamond. What now? You play the ♠AK and ruff a spade in dummy, discovering that West began with only two spades alongside his singleton trump. You then have to decide whether to draw trumps before playing on diamonds. You are in a good contract and want to stay ahead of those in 6NT, who will go one down unless clubs break 3-3. What will you do next?

If you draw all the trumps and then play a diamond, you will go down when East holds the ♢A and can cash several spades. What if you play on diamonds while you still hold some trumps to protect you against a spade continuation? You will then go down when West holds the ♢A and can give his partner a ruff in one of the minor suits. East began with six spades and four hearts. He is therefore certain to hold a minor-suit singleton. What is more, West holds ten minor-suit cards to East's three and is therefore a big favorite to hold the ♢A.

It's not a close decision. You should draw the remaining trumps and then play a diamond. West does indeed hold the ♢A and you score +1430 for what will be a splendid matchpoint score.

SUMMARY

- We saw in Chapter 13 that safety plays are generally a good idea at IMPs. When playing matchpoints, you often cannot afford a safety play that may cost you a valuable overtrick. However, if your contract is a good one that may not be widely bid, you are entitled to protect your good score by playing safely.

- Suppose you or your partner had a close decision whether to bid 6♠ or 6NT. If you decide or guess correctly and see that the other contract may be in trouble, consider making a safety play to guarantee success in your contract.

- Sometimes you are weak in a particular suit and are worried that this may put 3NT at risk. If you play in a major-suit game with a 5-2 or 4-3 fit instead, and see that 3NT was indeed likely to fail, you are entitled to use a safety play to guarantee your game.

Tᴇꜱᴛ Yᴏᴜʀꜱᴇʟꜰ

1.
    ♠ 5   Matchpoints
    ♡ 9 7
    ♢ 10 6 4
    ♣ A K J 9 6 5 3

    ♠ A K 9 7 4
    ♡ A K 6
    ♢ A K 3
    ♣ 4 2

West	North	East	South
	3♣	pass	4NT
pass	5♡	pass	6NT
all pass			

West leads the ♠J against 6NT at matchpoints. How will you play the contract?

2.
    ♠ A   Matchpoints
    ♡ K 8 5
    ♢ A Q J 10 5
    ♣ 8 7 5 2

    ♠ 8 6 5 3
    ♡ A Q 6 4 2
    ♢ K 7 6
    ♣ A

West	North	East	South
	1♢	pass	1♡
pass	2♡	pass	3♢
pass	3♠	pass	4NT
pass	5♠	pass	6♡
all pass			

West leads the ♠J against 6♡ at matchpoints. How will you play the contract?

ANSWERS

1.

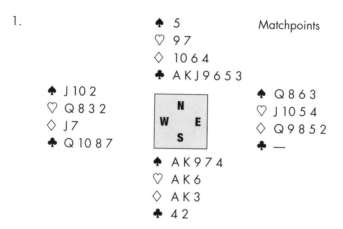

```
          ♠ 5             Matchpoints
          ♡ 9 7
          ◇ 10 6 4
          ♣ A K J 9 6 5 3

♠ J 10 2                      ♠ Q 8 6 3
♡ Q 8 3 2      N              ♡ J 10 5 4
◇ J 7       W     E           ◇ Q 9 8 5 2
♣ Q 10 8 7      S             ♣ —

          ♠ A K 9 7 4
          ♡ A K 6
          ◇ A K 3
          ♣ 4 2
```

West leads the ♠J against 6NT. There will be several pairs in 6♣ and others who do not bid a slam at all. Since +990 for twelve tricks in 6NT will beat +940 for thirteen tricks in 6♣, you should go all out to safeguard your slam. On the first round of clubs, cover West's ♣7 with the ♣9. If this loses to the ♣10 or ♣Q, you can claim the remaining tricks.

In a national final, with several pairs likely to be in 6NT, you might go for an overtrick by finessing the ♣J. You would go down on the layout shown, but make twelve or thirteen tricks, otherwise.

2.

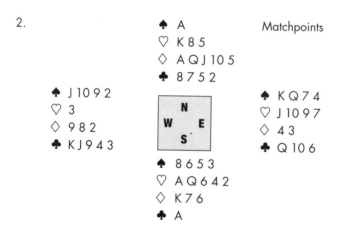

```
          ♠ A             Matchpoints
          ♡ K 8 5
          ◇ A Q J 10 5
          ♣ 8 7 5 2

♠ J 10 9 2                    ♠ K Q 7 4
♡ 3            N              ♡ J 10 9 7
◇ 9 8 2     W     E           ◇ 4 3
♣ K J 9 4 3     S             ♣ Q 10 6

          ♠ 8 6 5 3
          ♡ A Q 6 4 2
          ◇ K 7 6
          ♣ A
```

West leads the ♠J against 6♡. You have worked wonders to reach this slam. Much of the field will stop in game and you should therefore play safely for twelve tricks. At Trick 2 you should duck a round of trumps to guard against a 4-1 trump break. You can then win the return, take a spade ruff, draw trumps and score five diamond tricks, bringing home the slam.

17

Making Life Difficult

As declarer, you must seek to apply pressure on the defenders. There are more opportunities at matchpoints than at IMPs, because the defenders must be wary about conceding overtricks.

Playing the right card from equals

Many players go through their entire bridge careers playing the wrong card as declarer when they hold a KQ or AK combination. The general rule is that *declarer should play the higher card from equals*. This gives away less information to the defenders. Deals such as the following are commonplace:

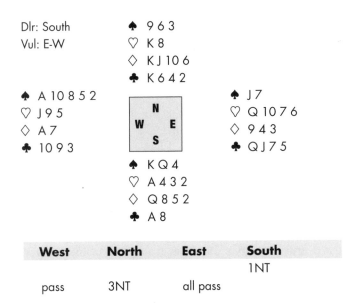

West	North	East	South
			1NT
pass	3NT	all pass	

West leads the ♠5 against 3NT and East plays the ♠J. Are you one of the millions of declarers who win with the ♠Q? It's the wrong card!

If you win with the ♠Q, West will know that you also hold the ♠K. Otherwise, East would have played the ♠K on the first trick. When West wins with the ◇A, he will switch to a club or a heart, unwilling to give you a second spade trick.

Now suppose that you know what you are doing and win with the ♠K at Trick 1. West will then have to guess whether to continue spades when he wins with the ◇A. If East holds the ♠Q, and correctly played the lower of equals from ♠QJ(x) at Trick 1, the defenders can claim four spade tricks and beat the contract.

Note that if West does decide to continue spades, which would not be the winning defense on this layout, he should play the ♠A next. This would pick up a bare ♠Q from East if he had started with ♠QJ doubleton. If instead East began with ♠QJx, he should unblock the ♠Q under West's ♠A, allowing partner to run the rest of the suit.

Creating doubt in the defender's mind

Sometimes you can tell, as declarer, the lie of the suit that has been led. Suppose East opens 1♡ and you arrive in 4♠. West leads the ♡3 and this is the lie of the suit:

```
              ♡ Q 10 2
   ♡ 3        [          ]      ♡ A K 9 7 6 4
              ♡ J 8 5
```

East's opening bid of 1♡ has promised at least five hearts, so you know that the ♡3 is a singleton. Suppose you play the ♡2 from dummy, as many players would, and East wins with the ♡K. It is not difficult for East to read the lie of the suit. If West had led from ♡J83, you would surely have played the ♡10 from dummy. Playing low instead is the action of a declarer who holds the ♡J. East will play a second top heart and deliver a ruff, beating the contract if the defenders have a further trick elsewhere.

To create an element of doubt in East's mind, you should play the ♡10 from dummy, just as you would if you held a singleton in the South hand. When East wins with the ♡K, he may be wary of cashing the ♡A, in case you ruff and dummy's ♡Q is set up as a winner. If East reads the position anyway and continues hearts, nothing has been lost. You tried your best.

This is a similar position:

```
              ♡ K 10 2
   ♡ 5        [          ]      ♡ A Q J 9 7 6 4
              ♡ 8 3
```

East opened 3♡ and you are playing in 4♠. West leads the ♡5, which is surely a singleton from your point of view. You play the ♡10 from dummy and East wins with the ♡J. If you follow with the ♡3, East can be certain how the heart suit lies. West would not have led the ♡5 from ♡85. East will duly cash the ♡A and play a third round of the suit.

Instead, you should follow with the ♡8. Now East must bear in mind that the lead may be from ♡53. If he continues with the ♡A in that case, you will ruff and dummy's ♡K will be established.

Much of the time these deceptive efforts will come to nothing. Particularly at IMPs, the defender may say to himself, 'Well, the best chance of beating the contract is that partner's lead is a singleton.' Now and again, though, the defenders will guess wrongly. Why not? They're only human.

Here is a final example of choosing the right card to mislead the defenders:

```
                    ♣ 10 9 6 4
      ♣ 2          [          ]        ♣ A 8 7 5 3
                    ♣ K Q J
```

East opened 1♣ and you are now playing in a major-suit game. West leads the ♣2, which you are fairly sure must be a singleton. East wins with the ♣A. Which card will you play from the South hand?

Some players will drop the ♣K, hoping that East thinks this is a singleton. Some hope! West would not have led the ♣2 from ♣QJ2. Following with the ♣J is no good either, since West would not have led the ♣2 from ♣KQ2. The only card that may cause East to doubt the situation is the ♣Q, since West might have led from ♣KJ2.

Feigning weakness at notrump

All too often, the defenders manage to attack your weakest suit when you are playing a notrump contract. Sometimes you are luckier and they lead a suit that you have well protected. It can then be a good idea to disguise your strength in that suit, to encourage the defenders to persist with their misdirected attack. Look at this deal:

```
Dlr: South          ♠ 9 8 4 2
Vul: E-W            ♡ 8 4
                    ◇ K 4 3
                    ♣ A K 7 5
♠ K 6 5                              ♠ A J 10 7
♡ Q 9 7 5 3          N               ♡ 10 6 2
◇ Q 9 7          W       E           ◇ 10 5
♣ 10 6               S               ♣ Q J 8 4
                    ♠ Q 3
                    ♡ A K J
                    ◇ A J 8 6 2
                    ♣ 9 3 2
```

West	North	East	South
			1NT
pass	2♣	pass	2◇
pass	3NT	all pass	

West leads the ♡5 against 3NT and East plays the ♡10. Suppose you do what comes naturally and win with the ♡J. With only seven top tricks, you need to establish the diamond suit. You cross to the ◇K and finesse the ◇J. West wins with the ◇Q and pauses to assess the situation. The play at Trick 1 marks you with the ♡AKJ. The best chance of beating the contract, from his point of view, will be a spade switch. The defenders pick up four spade tricks and you are one down.

Now see what may happen if you win the first trick with the ♡K. West is then likely to place his partner with ♡J10x. When he wins with the ◇Q he may well persist with hearts, aiming to set up the suit. Three hearts, four diamonds and two clubs will give you the game.

Leading towards the closed hand

It is not too difficult for a defender to find the right play when you are leading towards dummy. He can see the cards that lie over him. It's another matter when you lead towards your hand. With an unknown honor combination on his left, life may be tricky for the defender in second seat.

The declarer did well on this deal from a Pacific-Asia championship:

```
Dlr: East              ♠ K 8 7 2
Vul: E-W               ♡ 9
                       ◇ A 10 8 3
                       ♣ Q 8 7 3

♠ 5                  ┌─────────┐      ♠ Q 10
♡ 10 6 5 3           │    N    │      ♡ A K Q 8 7
◇ 7 6 5 4 2          │ W     E │      ◇ K Q J
♣ J 9 4              │    S    │      ♣ A K 10
                     └─────────┘
                       ♠ A J 9 6 4 3
                       ♡ J 4 2
                       ◇ 9
                       ♣ 6 5 2
```

West	North	East	South
Ho	Hua	Shen	Loo
		2♣	3♠
pass	4♠	pass	pass
dbl	all pass		

West led a heart to East's ♡Q and back came the ♠10. With the 2♣ opener sitting over the ♣Q, prospects of avoiding three club losers were slim. Would you have spotted any chance?

Declarer won the trump switch with the ♠J, crossed to the ♠K and led a low club towards his hand. You can see the problem that East faced. It seemed that declarer might hold the ♣J. He rose with the ♣K and switched to the ◇K, won with dummy's ◇A. Now declarer led another low club towards his hand. Again, East did not like to risk the possibility of declarer holding the ♣J. He went up with the ♣A and tried to cash a diamond. Curtains! Declarer ruffed the second diamond and claimed the contract.

The technique declarer used was 'leading towards the closed hand'. East had no idea what declarer held in clubs and it was not easy for him to find the right defense. Here it was the contract that was at stake. Just as often, at matchpoints, declarer may be seeking an overtrick or perhaps avoiding an extra undertrick. You can use the same deceptive play with this sort of holding:

```
                   ◇ K 8 7 2
◇ J 9 5            ▭▭▭▭▭▭        ◇ A 10 6 4
                   ◇ Q 3
```

When East has bid and you expect him to hold the ◇A, lead a low card from dummy. If he thinks you may hold the bare ◇Q, he might be tempted to rise with the ◇A. If instead he plays low and the ◇Q wins, cross to dummy and lead a second round of diamonds towards your hand. Now East may be worried that you started with ◇QJ doubleton. If he plays his ◇A unnecessarily, you will score two diamond tricks.

SUMMARY

- When you are declarer, it is generally right to win with the higher of two touching honors, to disguise your holding.

- By leading towards the closed hand, you can often cause a problem for the defender sitting in second seat. He may have to guess what honor cards (if any) you hold.

- When you suspect that the opening lead against a suit contract is a singleton, you can try to disguise this by 'hiding' a lower card in your hand. For example, West may lead a singleton ♣6. East wins with the ♣A and you play the ♣7 from ♣973. East must now allow for the fact that partner may have led from ♣63.

TEST YOURSELF

1.
$\spadesuit$ 9 5
$\heartsuit$ A K 8 4
$\diamondsuit$ Q 4 2
$\clubsuit$ J 10 7 5

$\spadesuit$ A Q 3
$\heartsuit$ Q J 2
$\diamondsuit$ 9 8
$\clubsuit$ A Q 9 3 2

West	North	East	South
			1NT
pass	2$\clubsuit$	pass	2$\diamondsuit$
pass	3NT	all pass	

West leads the $\spadesuit$6 against 3NT, East playing the $\spadesuit$J. How will you play the contract?

2.
$\spadesuit$ Q J 10 6
$\heartsuit$ A 7 2
$\diamondsuit$ A Q 6 5
$\clubsuit$ K 3

$\spadesuit$ A K 9 7 4
$\heartsuit$ K 9
$\diamondsuit$ 9 7 3 2
$\clubsuit$ A Q

West	North	East	South
			1$\spadesuit$
pass	2NT	pass	3NT
pass	6$\spadesuit$	all pass	

North employs the Jacoby 2NT and your rebid shows extra values and no shortage. West leads the $\spadesuit$2 against the spade slam. How will you play the contract?

ANSWERS

1.

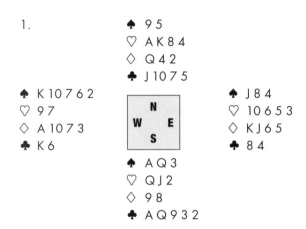

You bid to 3NT and West leads the ♠6 to East's ♠J. Suppose you win with the ♠Q, cross to the ♡A and run the ♣J. Knowing that you hold the ♠A, West may well try a diamond switch. The defenders will score four diamonds for one down. A better idea is to disguise your spade stopper by winning the first trick with the ♠A. You cross to the ♡A and run the ♣J. When West wins with the ♣K, he may continue with the ♠2, in the hope that East began with something like ♠QJ4. Ten tricks will result.

2.

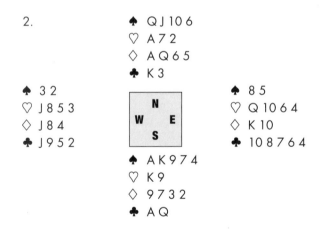

West leads a trump against 6♠. On the face of it, you will need to find diamonds 3-2 with West holding the ◇K. (An elimination play is no good; with your diamonds 4-4, the opponents could safely give a ruff-and-sluff.) Win with the ♠Q and immediately lead the ◇5 towards the closed hand. Many an East player will rise with the ◇K, fearful that you hold the ◇J. If East follows smoothly with a low card, you have lost nothing. You can finesse the ◇Q on the second round.

18

Accepting Defeat

Suppose you bid to a normal contract and run into a possibly fatal bad break. In a matchpoint event this is no cause for despair. The same thing will happen to many other declarers and a minus score will not necessarily give you a bad board. However, you must make sure not to suffer a bigger penalty than your rivals at the other tables.

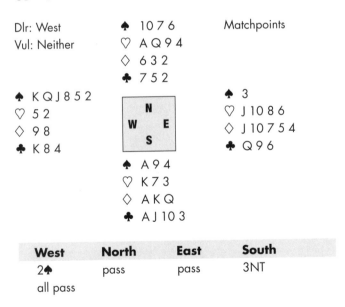

	Dlr: West	♠ 10 7 6		Matchpoints
	Vul: Neither	♡ A Q 9 4		
		◇ 6 3 2		
		♣ 7 5 2		
♠ K Q J 8 5 2			♠ 3	
♡ 5 2			♡ J 10 8 6	
◇ 9 8			◇ J 10 7 5 4	
♣ K 8 4			♣ Q 9 6	
		♠ A 9 4		
		♡ K 7 3		
		◇ A K Q		
		♣ A J 10 3		

West	North	East	South
2♠	pass	pass	3NT
all pass			

West leads the ♠K against your contract of 3NT. You win the second round of spades, as East discards a diamond. You can see eight top tricks and would like to score a fourth trick from the hearts. When you play three rounds of that suit, West discards a club on the third round. What now?

There is still a chance of making the contract. If East holds both the ♣K and ♣Q, you can establish at least one extra club trick and make the game. At IMPs, you should take almost any chance of making your game, since the potential gain will dwarf the cost of an extra undertrick. When you're playing this deal at matchpoints, the situation is different. Suppose you play a club to the ♣J and West wins with one of the missing honors. He will cash four more spade tricks and you will be two down. An extra minus 50 when the entire field is likely to be in 3NT will be costly indeed.

The chance of creating an extra club trick is massively under 50%; if you play on clubs, you will lose much more often than you will gain. Recalling that at matchpoints it is the frequency of gaining that is important, rather than the amount of the gain, you should simply take your eight top tricks and concede one down gracefully.

See what you make of this deal:

```
Dlr: North        ♠ Q J 8          Matchpoints
Vul: Both         ♡ K 4 2
                  ◇ A K J 8 2
                  ♣ Q 7

♠ 10 7 4                            ♠ 9 6 5 2
♡ J 9 8 3          N                ♡ —
◇ 9 7          W       E            ◇ Q 10 6 4
♣ 9 8 6 5          S                ♣ J 10 4 3 2

                  ♠ A K 3
                  ♡ A Q 10 7 6 5
                  ◇ 5 3
                  ♣ A K
```

West	North	East	South
	1NT	pass	3♡
pass	4◇	pass	4NT
pass	5♡	pass	5NT
pass	6◇	pass	7NT
all pass			

Your 3♡ response shows long hearts and suggests a slam. North's 4◇ agrees hearts and shows a diamond control, denying any control in the black suits. On finding him with two keycards and the ◇K, you are happy to bid 7NT.

West leads the ♣9 and you win in your hand. You place the ♡A on the table, preparing to claim the grand slam and — you call that justice? — East discards a club. How will you continue the play?

You are in an excellent contract and with these values you both hope and expect that most of the field will be in a grand slam. Is there any remaining chance of making thirteen tricks? Yes, if West holds ◇Qxx, you will be able to score five diamonds, three spades, three hearts and two clubs. That is only a 16% chance, however, when West is known to hold four hearts.

If you attempt to rescue yourself by finessing the ◇J (and then hoping for a 3-3 diamond break), you may end up two down instead of one down. Unless you are playing in a very poor field and expect that bidding this 95% grand slam will be beyond most of the competitors, you should give up a heart trick and concede one down. Remember that all the pairs in 7♡ instead of 7NT are certain to go one down.

At IMPs, of course, you would hasten to take the diamond finesse, happy to grab any chance of making +2220.

SUMMARY

- Suppose you reach a normal contract at matchpoints and subsequently suffer an unexpected bad break or adverse ruff that will probably defeat you. You should be wary of trying to rescue the contract when this is likely to put you two down instead of one down.

- There will be plenty of other competitors in the same contract, running into the same bad break. Do not fall behind them by playing for some 20% chance elsewhere.

- When you meet such a situation at IMPs, your approach will be entirely different. You are entitled to take more or less any chance of rescuing a game or slam contract.

TEST YOURSELF

1.   Dlr: South   ♠ 7 3   Matchpoints
      Vul: Both   ♡ Q J 5 4
                   ♢ 9 8 3
                   ♣ A Q J 8

                   ♠ A 5
                   ♡ K 10 6
                   ♢ A Q 10 7 6
                   ♣ K 6 2

West	North	East	South
			1NT
pass	2♣	pass	2♢
pass	3NT	all pass	

How will you play this matchpoint 3NT when West leads the ♠Q, East encouraging with the ♠9?

2.   Dlr: South   ♠ J 7 5   Matchpoints
      Vul: Neither   ♡ K 5
                   ♢ 10 9 8 6 4
                   ♣ Q 9 3

                   ♠ 4 2
                   ♡ A 10 8 4 2
                   ♢ 3 2
                   ♣ A K J 8

West	North	East	South
			1♡
pass	1NT	pass	2♣
pass	2♡	all pass	

West leads the ♠K and continues with the ♠6 to East's ♠A. You ruff the low spade continuation and play the ♡K and ♡A, West following with the ♡J on the second round. How will you continue?

ANSWERS

1.

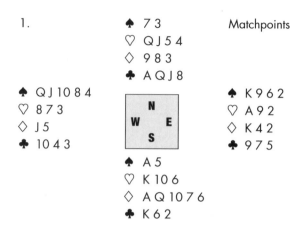

Matchpoints

West leads the ♠Q. To make 3NT, you need to find East with the ◇KJ. You would then score five diamond tricks and +630 for a top. This will happen only 24% of the time. When West holds one or both diamond honors (a 76% chance) you would go at least two down. The bidding and opening lead appear to be standard. You should therefore accept one down by establishing the heart suit.

2.

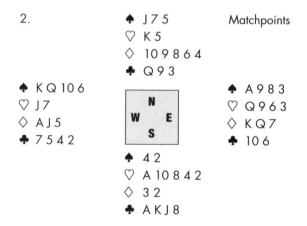

Matchpoints

West leads the ♠K against 2♡. You ruff the third spade and play the ♡K and ♡A, the ♡J appearing from West. If trumps are 3-3, you can play a third trump now, making the contract. However, West is more likely to hold ♡Jx or ♡Qx than ♡QJx (Restricted Choice). If you play another trump and they are 4-2, you will go three down (-150 against the possible −110 or −140 in 2♠ elsewhere.) You should abandon trumps and play on clubs, accepting −50 for one down.

PART III

DEFENSE TACTICS

19

Helping Partner in Defense

What should you do when partner makes a mistake during the defense? A tempting possibility is to glare at him, muttering, 'Not again!' Surprise, surprise, this is not the recommended tactic. He will regret the error (if indeed it was an error) as much as you do. A more constructive approach is to search for some way in which you could have made life easier for your partner, perhaps guiding him to a successful defense.

Helping partner with attitude signals

Suppose partner leads a high honor to the first trick, or he leads low and dummy plays the ace. In cases like these you have the chance to give an 'attitude signal'. A high card will encourage a continuation and a low card will discourage. When deciding how to signal, you may need to look beyond your holding in the suit that has been led. Take the East cards on this deal:

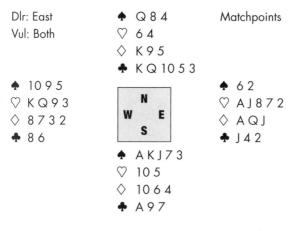

Dlr: East
Vul: Both

♠ Q 8 4
♡ 6 4
◇ K 9 5
♣ K Q 10 5 3

Matchpoints

♠ 10 9 5
♡ K Q 9 3
◇ 8 7 3 2
♣ 8 6

♠ 6 2
♡ A J 8 7 2
◇ A Q J
♣ J 4 2

♠ A K J 7 3
♡ 10 5
◇ 10 6 4
♣ A 9 7

West	North	East	South
		1♡	1♠
3♡	3♠	all pass	

With a four-card fit for your major suit and a bit of shape, West makes a preemptive raise to 3♡. (He would bid 2♠ with a sound raise to 3♡.) How will you defend when he leads the ♡K?

Holding the ♡A, you would usually signal encouragement with the ♡8. It is not the best idea here because you want partner to switch to diamonds. You should therefore discourage with the ♡2. It is clear from dummy's holdings that a diamond switch is a better bet than a club switch. West switches to the ◇8 (a high card to tell you that he holds no honor in the suit) and you win with the ◇J. You return to West's hand with a low heart to his ♡Q, and another diamond allows you to claim two more diamond tricks. The preemptive raise, combined with your accurate defense, will give you +100 and a good matchpoint score.

Helping partner with count signals

One of the most important weapons available to the defenders is the use of count signals. You play a high card to show an even number of cards in a suit, a low card to show an odd number. A count signal is vital on deals of this sort:

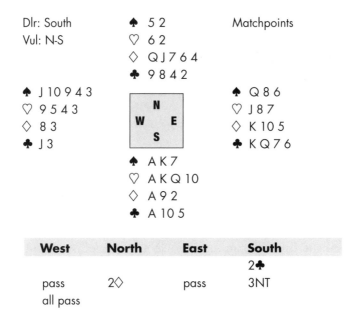

Dlr: South	♠ 5 2	Matchpoints
Vul: N-S	♡ 6 2	
	◇ Q J 7 6 4	
	♣ 9 8 4 2	

♠ J 10 9 4 3
♡ 9 5 4 3
◇ 8 3
♣ J 3

♠ Q 8 6
♡ J 8 7
◇ K 10 5
♣ K Q 7 6

♠ A K 7
♡ A K Q 10
◇ A 9 2
♣ A 10 5

West	North	East	South
			2♣
pass	2◇	pass	3NT
all pass			

You are sitting East, defending a matchpoint contract of 3NT. West leads the ♠J and you signal encouragement with the ♠8 (an attitude signal on partner's leads). Declarer wins with the ♠A and continues with the ◇A, followed by the ◇9 to dummy's ◇Q. How should you defend?

If declarer began with a doubleton ◇A9, you must win the trick. This will restrict declarer to only one diamond trick because the dummy will be dead. If instead declarer began with ◇A92, you must hold up the ◇K on the second round. How can you know which is the right action?

Your partner must show you how many diamonds he holds by giving a count signal. On this deal, he will play the ◇8 on the first round and then the ◇3. You will then place him with two diamonds, leaving three for declarer. By holding up the ◇K, you will restrict declarer to two diamond tricks, rather than four. He will still make nine tricks, thanks to the favorable heart lie, but +600 will be a poor score compared with the +660 that you would let through by winning the second round of diamonds.

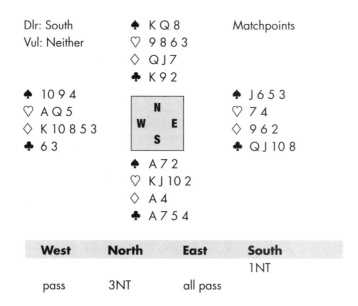

Dlr: South
Vul: Neither

♠ K Q 8
♡ 9 8 6 3
◇ Q J 7
♣ K 9 2

Matchpoints

♠ 10 9 4
♡ A Q 5
◇ K 10 8 5 3
♣ 6 3

♠ J 6 5 3
♡ 7 4
◇ 9 6 2
♣ Q J 10 8

♠ A 7 2
♡ K J 10 2
◇ A 4
♣ A 7 5 4

West	North	East	South
			1NT
pass	3NT	all pass	

With 4-3-3-3 shape, poor hearts and a healthy 11 points, North judges not to use Stayman. This is a good decision, as you can see. In 4♡, declarer would have lost two hearts, one diamond and a club.

Let's look at the defense against 3NT. Sitting West, you lead the ◇5. Dummy plays the ◇Q and your partner contributes the ◇2. Declarer then runs the ♡9 to your queen, partner playing the ♡7. What will you do then?

If declarer began with ◇A4, you would like to knock out the ◇A while you still hold the ♡A. If instead declarer started with ◇A64, you will give him an extra trick by persisting with diamonds. (Even if it's impossible to beat the contract, you will not want to present declarer with an overtrick at matchpoints.) How can you tell what to do?

Again your partner will assist you with a count signal. Even if you normally play attitude signals on partner's lead, as most players do, you should switch to count signals when your inability to beat dummy's card makes your attitude clear. Here, partner's ◇2 means that he holds either three diamonds or one. Since you can expect to beat the contract when partner holds three diamonds and South's ◇A is now bare, you continue diamonds. When declarer wins with the ace and plays another heart, you cash your diamond winners for one down.

(Note that partner's ♡7 was also a count signal, showing a doubleton. Since this marked declarer with four hearts, it increased the chance that he would hold two diamonds rather than four.)

Helping partner with a suit preference signal

Sometimes you make the opening lead and the appearance of dummy tells you that it will be unprofitable to persist with the suit. Perhaps you lead an ace and dummy holds the king-queen or a singleton in the suit. Since there is not much point in partner giving you either an attitude or count signal in the suit that was led, he should instead give a 'suit preference signal', suggesting which of the other side suits he holds more strongly. Look at this matchpoint deal:

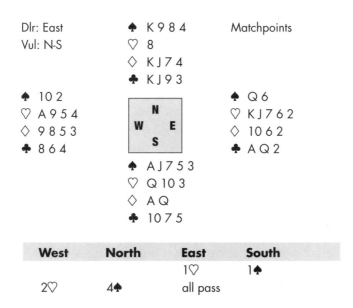

Dlr: East	♠ K 9 8 4	Matchpoints
Vul: N-S	♡ 8	
	◇ K J 7 4	
	♣ K J 9 3	

♠ 10 2
♡ A 9 5 4
◇ 9 8 5 3
♣ 8 6 4

♠ Q 6
♡ K J 7 6 2
◇ 10 6 2
♣ A Q 2

♠ A J 7 5 3
♡ Q 10 3
◇ A Q
♣ 10 7 5

West	North	East	South
		1♡	1♠
2♡	4♠	all pass	

Sitting West, you lead the ♡A. When dummy has a singleton heart, there would be little merit in an attitude or count signal from partner. His ♡2 is a suit preference signal. A *high* spot card would suggest a switch to the *higher* remaining side suit; a *low* spot card suggests the *lower* suit.

You duly switch to a club and partner claims two tricks in the suit, holding declarer to +620. Without a club switch, declarer would discard two clubs on the diamonds and pick up +650 for a shared top.

Take the East cards here, looking for an opportunity to help your partner.

```
Dlr: North      ♠ J 10 9 6      Matchpoints
Vul: N-S        ♡ Q 6
                ◇ Q 9 5
                ♣ A K Q 8

♠ A 7                           ♠ 4 2
♡ K 8 5 4 3         N           ♡ A J 7 2
◇ J 10 4 3 2    W       E       ◇ 8 7
♣ 3                 S           ♣ J 9 6 5 2

                ♠ K Q 8 5 3
                ♡ 10 9
                ◇ A K 6
                ♣ 10 7 4
```

West	North	East	South
	1♣	pass	1♠
pass	2♠	pass	4♠
all pass			

West, your partner, leads the ♣3 against the spade game. Dummy wins with the ♣Q and you must now be awake. Partner's ♣3, a lead of dummy's suit, is surely a singleton. You must hope that he will gain the lead in trumps, and he will then need to know how to reach your hand for a club ruff. Tell him the answer! Follow with the ♣9 at Trick 1. This would be no use to man or beast if it was an attitude or count signal. It can only be a suit preference signal, suggesting a heart return rather than a diamond.

Partner duly wins the first round of trumps and returns the ♡4. (He would have been reluctant to lead away from a king, with the queen in dummy, unless you had given such a clear suit preference signal.) You win with the ♡A and give partner a club ruff. West's ♡K then puts the game one down.

Suppose declarer had held four diamonds and only one heart. Your excellent defense would then have been necessary to stop him from scoring a precious matchpoint overtrick.

Showing partner where your tricks are

Would you have made life easy for your partner on this deal?

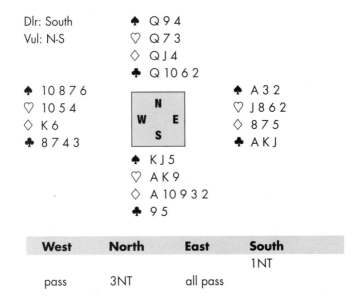

Dlr: South
Vul: N-S

```
                  ♠ Q 9 4
                  ♡ Q 7 3
                  ◇ Q J 4
                  ♣ Q 10 6 2
♠ 10 8 7 6                        ♠ A 3 2
♡ 10 5 4            N             ♡ J 8 6 2
◇ K 6          W       E          ◇ 8 7 5
♣ 8 7 4 3          S             ♣ A K J
                  ♠ K J 5
                  ♡ A K 9
                  ◇ A 10 9 3 2
                  ♣ 9 5
```

West	North	East	South
			1NT
pass	3NT	all pass	

You are sitting East and your partner leads the ♠6, dummy playing low. What is your plan for the defense?

Suppose you return the ♠3 at Trick 2. Declarer wins with dummy's ♠Q and runs the ◇Q to West's ◇K. It will be an agonizing moment for you as partner considers what to do next. You know that a club switch will beat the contract, but he does not. If partner plays another spade or switches to a heart, declarer will claim nine tricks for the contract.

What could you have done to assist your partner? It's not too difficult — you should cash the ♣K before returning a spade. When partner wins the lead (either in spades or diamonds, from your point of view), he will know that you would like a club return.

On the bidding that we showed, this helpful defense will put 3NT one down. Suppose the opponents had stopped in 2NT, playing matchpoints. The same defense would then assist you in preventing an overtrick.

SUMMARY

- Defense can be difficult and quite often you or your partner may be forced to guess what to do. You must take every opportunity to assist each other to make the right decisions.

- Signaling is an important part of defense. Remember that such signals are intended to tell partner something useful about your hand. They are not meant to tell him what to do! How can you possibly know that, when you can see only your own hand and not his?

- When partner leads to a trick and your attitude is obvious, perhaps because of dummy's cards in the suit, you should give a count signal instead. You should also signal count on declarer's suits, unless you think that this will help declarer more than your partner.

- When neither attitude nor count signals would be of any use to partner, you will have the opportunity to give a suit preference signal. A common situation arises when dummy's cards make it clear that there can be no value in a continuation of the suit led.

TEST YOURSELF

1.

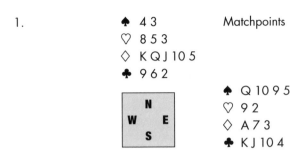

♠	4 3
♡	8 5 3
◇	K Q J 10 5
♣	9 6 2

Matchpoints

	♠	Q 10 9 5
	♡	9 2
	◇	A 7 3
	♣	K J 10 4

West	North	East	South
			1♣
pass	1◇	pass	2NT
pass	3NT	all pass	

Your partner, West, leads the ♡6 to your ♡9 and South's ♡J. When declarer leads the ◇4, West follows with the ◇2, and you allow the ◇K to win (aiming to cut declarer off from the dummy). How will you continue the defense when the ◇Q is led from dummy at Trick 3?

2.

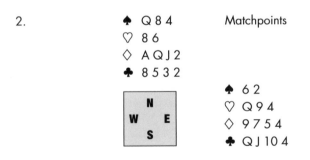

♠	Q 8 4
♡	8 6
◇	A Q J 2
♣	8 5 3 2

Matchpoints

	♠	6 2
	♡	Q 9 4
	◇	9 7 5 4
	♣	Q J 10 4

West	North	East	South
1♡	pass	2♡	2♠
3♡	3♠	pass	4♠
all pass			

Your partner, West, leads the ♡A against the spade game. What is your plan for the defense?

ANSWERS

1.

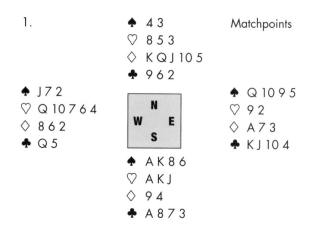

Matchpoints

Defending 3NT, partner leads the ♡6 to your ♡9 and South's ♡J. When the ◇4 is led, partner follows with the ◇2 and you allow dummy's ◇K to win. How should you defend when the ◇Q is led? If declarer started with only two diamonds, you should take your ◇A now; otherwise, he will score an undeserved second diamond trick. If instead declarer has three diamonds, you must hold up for one more round. Partner's ◇2 is a count signal, showing an odd number of diamonds. So take the ◇A and return a heart. The contract will go two down for an excellent matchpoint score.

2.

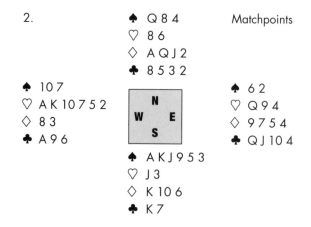

Matchpoints

Defending 4♠, partner leads the ♡A. You place him with the ♡AK and should signal encouragement with the ♡9. Placing you with the ♡Q, West leads a low heart next. You win with the ♡Q and a switch to the ♣Q produces two club tricks, beating the contract. After any other defense, declarer would draw trumps and discard a club on dummy's diamonds.

20

OPENING LEADS AT NOTRUMP

What is your objective when you choose an opening lead against 3NT, playing IMPs? Right, you want to beat the contract! At matchpoint pairs, you would still *like* to beat the contract, but it is equally important that you do not give away an unnecessary overtrick when 3NT cannot be beaten by any lead.

The recently-published *Winning Notrump Leads* (by David Bird and Taf Anthias) gives an in-depth analysis of which opening leads are best, at both IMPs and matchpoints. As an introduction to this chapter, let's look at just one result from that book. The opponents' bidding is 1NT–3NT. What opening lead would you choose from this hand?

♠ J 8 6   ♡ 9 5   ◇ K Q 7 2   ♣ K J 7 2

These were the results (determined by computer simulation):

	Beats contract (IMPs)	Average Tricks (Matchpoints)
♠6	21.3%	3.43
♡9	20.6%	3.41
◇2	14.1%	3.16
♣2	15.7%	3.25

Just this one hand can teach you an enormous amount about opening leads at notrump! Leading from one of the short major suits is much better than leading from an honor-laden four-card minor suit. This is true at both IMPs and matchpoint pairs. As you see, leading the ♠6 will beat 3NT 21.3% of the time. Leading the ♣2 gives you only a 15.7% chance. At matchpoints, where the average number of defensive tricks is the important measure, again the ♠6 is the best lead. It will give you an average of 3.43 defensive tricks against only 3.25 for a club lead.

Now we must ask: Why do the major-suit leads do better? There are two good reasons. First of all, the fact that the responder did not bid Stayman or use a transfer bid, suggests that he is longer in the minors than in the majors. (On this auction the defenders will hold between them an average of 7.2 cards in each major suit, only 5.8 cards in each minor suit.) Secondly, there is no reason to think that leading from four cards headed by one or two honors will be a good lead. On average, it costs about half a trick to lead away from an honor. This may be worthwhile if you are leading from a five-card suit (♣KJ752) because you have a fair prospect of developing some long cards in the suit. It is much less worthwhile when you hold only a four-card suit (♣KJ72).

The table on the previous page shows that with this particular West hand, which contains no bad breaks for declarer, 3NT will go down only one time in five. You do not want to surrender an unnecessary overtrick at matchpoints on the other four deals in five. That is why a passive lead (for example from three low cards) is a better prospect than an aggressive one from a four-card suit headed by one or two honors.

> **THINK ABOUT...**
>
> *It is not usually a good idea to lead from a six-card suit of no particular strength (such as ◇K108652). The odds are high that partner has only a singleton. If he has a singleton ◇Q, declarer can hold up the ace. Five-card suits make the best leads from length.*

Leading from a weak hand

When your own hand is weak, it can be a waste of time leading your own best suit. Even if you happen to find partner with a useful honor or two and can set up the suit, you will have no entry to enjoy the long cards. In such a situation, you should lead a short suit, hoping to hit partner's length. When your shortage is in a major suit, this can be a very good chance. Suppose the bidding goes 1NT-3NT and you have to find a lead from:

♠ 10 8 7 5 2   ♡ J 9   ◇ 10 4   ♣ J 10 9 7

You have five spades, albeit weak ones, and a sequence in clubs. Will you lead one of the black suits or something different?

The ♡J is the best lead at both IMPs and matchpoints! It gives you a 19.5% chance of beating the contract. The next best lead (the ♠5) offers only a 14.4% chance. With responder making no effort to find a major-suit fit, you partner is quite likely to hold five hearts. What is more, he will have some outside high cards to act as entries.

After the same auction (1NT-3NT) what would you lead from this hand?

♠ A 3   ♡ 9 6 5   ◇ 10 6 4 3 2   ♣ 7 6 5

Don't think only of your own hand. What sort of hand does partner hold? It is quite likely that he holds around 10 points including a five-card spade suit. He may have something like:

♠ Q 10 7 6 2   ♡ A 8 2   ◇ 9 5   ♣ Q J 8

THINK ABOUT...

A lead from a low doubleton or tripleton can work well because you are **leading towards** *whatever honors partner may hold. Consider such a lead when your own hand is weak. As always, prefer a major suit to a minor suit when responder made no effort to find a major-suit fit.*

If your partner was on lead, he would try his luck with the ♠6. You would win with the ♠A and return the suit, with a good chance of beating the contract. So, lead the ♠A. Your partner will think he is playing with Superman!

(The computer simulation shows that the ♠A lead will beat the contract 20.5% of the time and is easily best at matchpoints too. A heart lead is next best, but succeeds only 12.8% of the time.)

Combining safety with aggression

You will often have to make a choice between a passive lead and an aggressive one (from a suit containing one or more honors). Sometimes, though, you have a chance to combine these aims. Suppose the bidding goes 1NT-3NT and you have to find a lead from:

♠ Q J 10 4   ♡ 8 3   ◇ A 10 8 5 3   ♣ J 6

You have a good five-card diamond suit headed by the ace, which may serve as an entry to enjoy any long cards that you can establish. Should you lead the ◇5 or the safer ♠Q?

The ♠Q is a massive winner, both at IMPs and matchpoints. This is partly because you should favor major-suit leads when the opponents have not used Stayman or a transfer bid. Suppose you are playing matchpoints and lead a low diamond. On average, you are surrendering almost half a trick each time! This is an enormous amount.

You may wonder what the best lead is from:

♠ A 10 8 5 3   ♡ 8 3   ◇ Q J 10 4   ♣ J 6

The queen from a sequence is still best at matchpoints, but the ♠5 is a big winner at IMPs. Again, this is because you should generally favor a major-suit lead when responder has shown no interest in a major suit (no Stayman, no transfer bid).

Leading against 6NT

Whatever your normal style may be when leading against a suit slam, it is essential to make a **passive lead against 6NT**. Why is that? It's because the declaring side is likely to hold a higher point count than when they bid a suit slam. If you unwisely lead from a suit such as ◇K1073, it is very likely indeed that declarer and the dummy between them will hold the ace and queen. You will often be giving away an extra trick — perhaps the trick that will allow 6NT to be made!

Suppose the opponents bid 1NT-6NT and you have to find an opening lead from one of these hands:

(a)	♠ 9	(b)	♠ J 7 4
	♡ 7 5 4		♡ 10 6 5
	◇ Q J 6 4		◇ Q 10 8 6 2
	♣ K 9 8 4 2		♣ 9 2

From hand (a) it would quite awful to lead from one of the minor suits. Declarer might easily hold something like ◇A105 opposite ◇K93. A diamond lead would then give three tricks in the suit. The ♠9 is not entirely safe because it might help declarer to pick up partner's ♠Q or ♠J. Best is the ♡7 (top of nothing).

From (b) a diamond lead is easily worst, both at matchpoints and IMPs. You must choose a passive lead against 6NT. A diamond lead will beat the notrump slam 4% of the time. A lead from any of the other suits will give you a 9-10% chance. Note that leading from a jack is not particularly dangerous, despite what some players say. If declarer holds ♠K93 opposite ♠AQ6, three spade tricks are his anyway. With ♠Q82 opposite ♠AK105, the suit was breaking 3-3 anyway.

The bidding is the same, 1NT-6NT, and you must choose a lead from these two hands:

(c)
♠ 8 5
♡ 10 6 4 3
♢ K Q 2
♣ 9 6 4 3

(d)
♠ Q 9 8 7 2
♡ J 9 6 5 3
♢ K 8 4
♣ —

Either black-suit lead is fine from (c). A heart lead is not far behind, but leading the ♢K would be a poor idea at both IMPs and matchpoints. Your partner will hold an ace only if they have bid 6NT on just 31 HCPs. If you lead a diamond honor, your partner might occasionally win a trick with a king in some other suit and then return a diamond (in your dreams, anyway). Meanwhile, there is a considerable risk that a diamond lead will give away an extra trick, perhaps declarer's twelfth trick.

On hand (d) you are forced to lead away from an honor. Which is the safest lead? Leading away from a jack is not as dangerous as leading from a king or queen; it is almost as safe as leading from spot cards. When you hold five hearts, declarer is not so likely to hold four hearts in either hand. If he has ♡AQ8 opposite ♡K104, for example, the lead will be safe. Computer simulation shows that a heart lead will beat 6NT 11% of the time, a spade lead 7% and a diamond lead 6%. A heart lead is best at matchpoints, too.

> **THINK ABOUT...**
>
> *The recommendation to make a safe lead against 6NT applies with even greater force when leading against 7NT.*

- When the opponents bid to 3NT, there may be only a small chance that you can beat the contract. At matchpoints, you should be wary of giving away an overtrick by making a risky lead from a suit such as ♠K1072 or ◇Q754.

- When you hold a five-card suit headed by one or more honors (♣KJ763 or ◇A9843), this represents a good opening lead. You run the same risk that your lead will give away a trick initially, but you have the compensation that you may be able to set up the suit and score several tricks.

- When your own hand is weak, it may be a waste of time to lead from your longest suit. Even if you could establish it, you would not have an entry to enjoy the long cards. Prefer to lead a short suit, hoping to find partner's length.

- When the auction is 1NT-3NT, favor a major-suit lead rather than one from a minor suit.

- Choose a passive lead against 6NT, at both IMPs and matchpoints. The opponents are likely to hold at least 32 points. If you make an attacking lead from a holding such as ♡KJ82, you are less likely to find partner with the ace or queen than you would be against a suit slam.

TEST YOURSELF

1. (a) ♠ A 7　　(b) ♠ 10 2　　(c) ♠ Q 8 6 5
　　 ♡ 8 5　　　　 ♡ K Q J 8　　 ♡ Q J 3
　　 ◇ K J 9 6 3　 ◇ A 10 6 4 3 2　◇ K 10 8 5 2
　　 ♣ A 10 7 2　　♣ 8　　　　 ♣ 9

The bidding is 1NT–3NT. What will you lead from each of these hands? Would it make any difference if it was IMPs or matchpoints?

2. (a) ♠ 9 5 3 2　　(b) ♠ 7 6 5 3　　(c) ♠ K Q 5
　　 ♡ J 4 2　　　 ♡ Q 7　　　　 ♡ 8 5 3
　　 ◇ 10 7　　　 ◇ Q 10 9 7 5 4 3　◇ 10 4
　　 ♣ J 6 5 3　　 ♣ —　　　　 ♣ J 9 5 3 2

The bidding is 1NT-3NT. What will you lead from each of these hands? Would it make any difference if it was IMPs or matchpoints?

3. (a) ♠ 9 7 6 5　　(b) ♠ 4 2　　(c) ♠ Q 10 7 2
　　 ♡ K J 8 2　　 ♡ 9 7　　　 ♡ J 9 7 6
　　 ◇ 8 5　　　　 ◇ K Q 9 5　 ◇ K 9 8 3
　　 ♣ K 7 3　　　 ♣ 10 9 8 7 3　♣ 2

The bidding is 1NT–6NT. What will you lead from each of these hands? Would it make any difference if it was IMPs or matchpoints?

ANSWERS

1. Hand (a) is perfect for an attacking lead of the ♢6. Even though you may give away a trick initially, you have two aces as later entries. There will be a great chance of scoring three or four diamonds, plus the two aces.

    On (b) the ♡K is the best lead (at both IMPs and matchpoints) by a *mile*! Remember that a moderate six-card suit is rarely a good lead against 3NT. Your partner will very often hold a singleton in the suit. (The ♡K gives you a 42% chance of beating 3NT, the ♢4 only 25%.)

    On (c), even though major-suit leads work well against an auction of 1NT-3NT, you should not lead from ♠Q865. Remember that four-card suits headed by one or two honors are not usually attractive. Leading from ♢K10852 may look good, but partner will often hold only one or two diamonds, and you do not have much by way of outside entries. Easily best (confirmed by computer simulation) is the queen from ♡QJ3.

2. Hand (a) is very weak and you should lead a short suit, aiming to find partner's length. As always, against 1NT-3NT, a major-suit lead is likely to be best. The ♡2 is your best shot, with a spade second best (same for both IMPs and matchpoints).

    A diamond lead is a waste of time from hand (b). Partner is probably void in the suit and you may give away a trick. Easily best from this weak hand is the ♡Q (at both IMPs and matchpoints).

    Hand (c) is fairly weak, and you should look for partner's length. The ♠K is clearly the best lead. It will give you a 21% chance of beating the contract, compared with a heart (15%) or a club (14%). The biggest advantage for a spade lead comes at matchpoints, where you can expect to score 3.3 tricks per deal, compared with 2.9 and 2.8 for the heart and club leads.

3. (a) A heart or club lead would be far too risky, at either IMPs or matchpoints. A spade lead is marginally better than a diamond because you have four cards in the suit. (A spade lead will beat 6NT 14% of the time; a heart lead will beat it 2% if the time! You hold 7 points, so partner will hold the ♡Q only if they have bid 6NT on 31 points.)

Are you tempted to lead the ◇K from (b), hoping that East will win a trick and then be able to return a diamond? Computer simulation shows that the ◇K lead is less likely to beat 6NT than a lead from any of the other suits. It may give away a trick when declarer has, say, ◇J64 opposite his ◇A107. A club lead is marginally ahead of the major-suit leads, but any passive lead is fine.

From (c), the ♡6 is the safest and best of the leads from the three four-card suits. It is unthinkable to lead from a king or a queen. However, the singleton ♣2 is best at both IMPs and matchpoints.

21

Should I Make a Risky Switch?

When you are defending at IMPs, you will seize any chance to beat the contract. It scarcely matters if you give away an overtrick worth 20 or 30 because the reward for beating, say, a game contract is several hundred points. The situation is quite different at matchpoints, where surrendering an overtrick in some commonly bid contract may cost the defenders half a top. In this chapter we will look at some deals where you have to assess the risk of giving declarer an overtrick.

```
Dlr: South          ♠ J 10 3              Matchpoints
Vul: Neither        ♡ J 8 3
                    ◇ K Q 6 4
                    ♣ K 6 3

♠ 9 8 7 4                              ♠ A 2
♡ 9 7 6          N                     ♡ A Q 10 5
◇ J 9 2       W      E                 ◇ 10 8 3
♣ J 9 7          S                     ♣ Q 8 5 2

                    ♠ K Q 6 5
                    ♡ K 4 2
                    ◇ A 7 5
                    ♣ A 10 4
```

West	North	East	South
			1NT
pass	3NT	all pass	

You are sitting East, playing in a matchpoint event, and your partner leads the ♠9 against 3NT. How will you defend?

If partner holds the ♡K, you can win the spade lead and switch to a low heart. Even if he holds only ♡Kx, you will be able to claim four heart tricks and beat the contract. How likely is that, though? The closed hands, between them, contain 18 points. So, if South holds a minimum of 15 points, there is just room for your partner to hold the ♡K. A 5000-

deal computer simulation (with the North and East hands fixed, South holding a random 1NT opener including the ♠KQ) reveals that West has a 21% chance of holding the ♡K.

There is a worthwhile chance of beating the contract and you would head for it immediately when playing IMPs. At matchpoints, a heart switch will give declarer an extra trick whenever he holds the ♡K (79%) and at least three cards in the suit (70% of 79%). He will run the switch to the ♡J and, when West cannot produce the ♡A on the first round, subsequently lead towards the ♡K. This will happen more than 50% of the time, way more often than the times that a heart switch will beat the contract. You should not, therefore, make such a risky switch at matchpoints.

Judging whether a switch is risky or not

Sometimes a switch looks risky, but you can see that you might as well go for it because declarer is likely to discard potential losers in the key suit anyway.

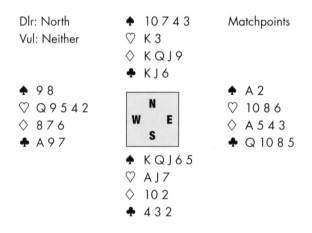

Dlr: North
Vul: Neither

Matchpoints

	♠ 10 7 4 3	
	♡ K 3	
	◇ K Q J 9	
	♣ K J 6	

♠ 9 8		♠ A 2
♡ Q 9 5 4 2	N	♡ 10 8 6
◇ 8 7 6	W E	◇ A 5 4 3
♣ A 9 7	S	♣ Q 10 8 5

	♠ K Q J 6 5	
	♡ A J 7	
	◇ 10 2	
	♣ 4 3 2	

West	**North**	**East**	**South**
	1◇	pass	1♠
pass	2♠	pass	4♠
all pass			

West leads the ♠9 and you win with the ♠A in the East seat. How should you continue the defense, bearing in mind that it is matchpoints?

If partner holds the ♣A, it may be possible to set up two club tricks before your ◇A is knocked out. South's bidding suggests that he holds something close to an opening bid. Even though you can already place him with the ♠KQJ, he is more likely than West to hold the ♣A. Switching from the ♣Q into dummy's ♣KJ tenace may then give declarer an extra club trick. Is it likely to cost, though? If you return a passive trump instead, declarer will establish the diamond suit. In the case where he began with ♣Axx, he will surely be able to discard his losing club on a surplus diamond winner.

Even if you judge that the chance of partner holding the ♣A is only around 30%, you should go ahead and make the risky club switch. As the cards lie, West will win and return the ♣9. The contract will then go one down. Declarer may even rise with the ♣K on the second round, draw the remaining trumps, play the ♡K and take a desperation finesse of the ♡J. (Since he does not expect many Easts to find your sharp defense, this would not be an unreasonable line of play.) The contract will then go two down!

On the next deal, you sit East and are able to build an accurate picture of the closed hands before making the key decision.

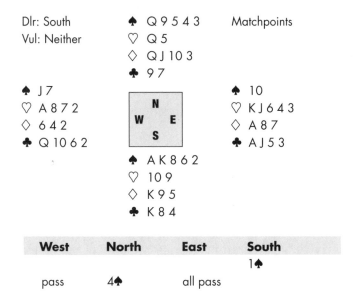

Dlr: South	♠ Q 9 5 4 3	Matchpoints
Vul: Neither	♡ Q 5	
	◇ Q J 10 3	
	♣ 9 7	

♠ J 7
♡ A 8 7 2
◇ 6 4 2
♣ Q 10 6 2

♠ 10
♡ K J 6 4 3
◇ A 8 7
♣ A J 5 3

♠ A K 8 6 2
♡ 10 9
◇ K 9 5
♣ K 8 4

West	**North**	**East**	**South**
			1♠
pass	4♠	all pass	

West leads the ♣2 against the spade game. A surprisingly light dummy appears and you win with the ♣A. When you return the ♣3, South wins with the ♣K and draws trumps with the ace and king. You discard a heart. How will you defend when declarer then leads the ◇5 to West's ◇2 and dummy's ◇Q?

North took quite a view, leaping to 4♠ on three queens and a jack. West has shown up with the ♣J already, and doubtless holds the ♣Q too. (If declarer held that card, he would be able to discard a heart from dummy.) Because of North's unusual action in the bidding, it is possible that partner holds the ♡A, and the contract is down on top tricks. Should you risk a heart switch?

You have little idea of South's point count. Making a risky switch is not justified just because dummy has overbid. South may well hold the ♡A and you will not want to give away an overtrick with a heart switch when most of the field may then be in 4♠.

On this deal, however, you can read the cards very accurately. West's ♣2 lead and his ◇2 count signal suggest that South's shape is 5=2=3=3. He is likely to hold the ◇K; otherwise, partner should have risen with the ◇K and switched to a heart (to establish a trick for your possible ♡KJ before the ◇A was knocked out). So, declarer will have a heart discard on the fourth round of diamonds. On this basis, a heart switch cannot give a trick away. A further consideration is that South might have opened 1NT with two aces and three kings. You duly collect two heart tricks before declarer can ditch one of his losers in the suit. The game goes down and a good board is yours.

SUMMARY

- When you are defending at IMPs, you must grab any chance of defeating the contract, particularly a game or a slam. If your attempt fails and allows declarer to make an overtrick, this hardly matters at all. You can afford a bundle of extra 20s and 30s in exchange for the big numbers you save by defeating a game or slam.

- The situation is different at matchpoints. If you make a risky switch, hoping to beat an impregnable contract, you may give declarer an otherwise impossible overtrick. This can cost you half a top.

- Unless declarer may be able to discard potential losers after a passive defense, do not risk an against-the-odds switch that is likely to cost a trick when unsuccessful.

- Do not make a risky switch just because the dummy has overbid and the contract may not be a common one. If declarer's bidding did not limit his hand, he may hold the high card that you hope your partner holds.

Test Yourself

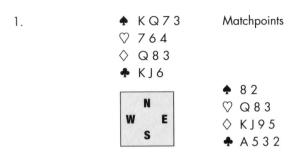

1.
    ♠ K Q 7 3
    ♡ 7 6 4
    ◇ Q 8 3
    ♣ K J 6
    Matchpoints

    ♠ 8 2
    ♡ Q 8 3
    ◇ K J 9 5
    ♣ A 5 3 2

West	North	East	South
			1♠
pass	3♠	pass	4♠
all pass			

Your partner, West, leads the ♣10 and dummy plays the ♣6. You win with the ♣A and South follows with the ♣4. What will you return at Trick 2?

2.
    ♠ 8 5 3
    ♡ K 4
    ◇ 10 4 2
    ♣ A Q J 6 3
    Matchpoints

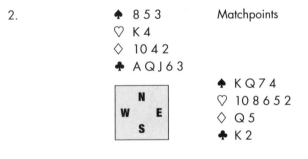

    ♠ K Q 7 4
    ♡ 10 8 6 5 2
    ◇ Q 5
    ♣ K 2

West	North	East	South
			1NT
pass	3NT	all pass	

Your partner, West, leads the ◇6 to your ◇Q, winning the first trick. What will you return at Trick 2?

ANSWERS

1.

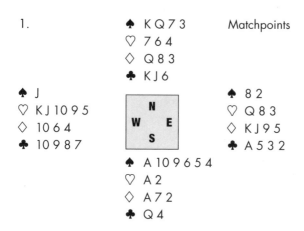

          ♠ K Q 7 3   Matchpoints
          ♡ 7 6 4
          ◇ Q 8 3
          ♣ K J 6

♠ J   ♠ 8 2
♡ K J 10 9 5   ♡ Q 8 3
◇ 10 6 4   ◇ K J 9 5
♣ 10 9 8 7   ♣ A 5 3 2

          ♠ A 10 9 6 5 4
          ♡ A 2
          ◇ A 7 2
          ♣ Q 4

Against 4♠, West leads the ♣10 to your ace. A diamond switch gives you the chance of a 'quick kill' if partner has the ◇A. What is the chance of West holding the ◇A, with the cards that you can see? A computer simulation makes it 31%. To score three diamond tricks, you would also need South to hold three or four diamonds. On this typical layout, the risky diamond switch will concede 650, giving you a very poor score. Switch to the ♡3 instead.

2.

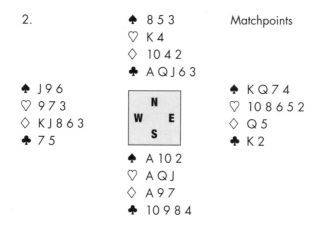

          ♠ 8 5 3   Matchpoints
          ♡ K 4
          ◇ 10 4 2
          ♣ A Q J 6 3

♠ J 9 6   ♠ K Q 7 4
♡ 9 7 3   ♡ 10 8 6 5 2
◇ K J 8 6 3   ◇ Q 5
♣ 7 5   ♣ K 2

          ♠ A 10 2
          ♡ A Q J
          ◇ A 9 7
          ♣ 10 9 8 4

Against 3NT, West leads the ◇6 to your ◇Q. South probably holds the ◇A, since it would be too dangerous to hold up from ◇Kxx. If you return a diamond, declarer will win and take a club finesse to your king. He will then have nine tricks. Although a low spade switch at Trick 2 may cost an overtrick, you should go for it! When partner holds the ♠J, you have a good chance of setting up three spades to defeat 3NT. If declarer holds ♠AJ9, he may finesse the ♠9 to West's ♠10, again ending in defeat.

22

Opening Leads against Suit Contracts

In the chapter on leads at notrump, we noted that the principle aim of an opening lead at IMPs is to beat the contract. It's a sad fact of life that most of the opponents' contracts cannot be beaten on any opening lead. At matchpoints it is therefore imperative that you do not give away unnecessary overtricks by making speculative leads away from an honor.

Winning Suit Contract Leads (by David Bird and Taf Anthias) gives an in-depth analysis of which opening leads are best at both IMPs and matchpoints. As before, we will begin this chapter with an instructive result from the book. The opponents' bidding is 1♠-2♠-4♠. What opening lead would you choose from this hand?

♠ 7 4 2 ♡ K J 9 7 ◇ Q 10 9 ♣ 10 5 2

These were the computer simulation results:

	Beats contract (IMPs)	Average Tricks (Matchpoints)
♠2	18.3%	2.65
♡7	10.8%	2.43
◇10	14.7%	2.50
♣2	16.2%	2.57

As you see, the two aggressive leads in the red suits fill the bottom places, both at IMPs and matchpoints. They are too likely to give a trick away! Leads from a king are the most risky, followed by leads from a queen. You might think that leading from a king-jack combination was a fair proposition, one likely to succeed if you found partner with the ace or the queen (I did, for thirty-five years!). In fact, it is the very worst of the leads from a king; you pay a double price because you are leading from the jack as well as from the king.

Leading from a ten (or a jack) is safer than leading from a higher honor. From this particular West hand, a trump lead is best. That's not because it is likely to fulfill any constructive purpose, such as stopping a ruff. It is because you greatly reduce the risk of giving a trick away.

Remember that aggressive leads from an honor, or two non-touching honors, are not generally a good idea (either at matchpoints or at IMPs).

Leading from shortage

Is it a good idea to lead a side-suit singleton? Yes, indeed! It is one of the very best leads you can make — just about as good as that Holy Grail of opening leads, an ace-king combination. The main intention of making such a lead is to allow partner to give you a ruff at some stage. However, the lead may work well merely because you are leading towards an honor combination in your partner's hand.

Suppose again that the bidding has been 1♠-2♠-4♠ and you must select a lead from this hand:

♠ 10 6   ♡ K Q J 6 5 2   ◇ 3   ♣ 9 8 7 4

Would you lead the ♡K or the singleton ◇3?

The singleton diamond is easily best! It will give you a 31% chance of beating the contract, compared with 21% for the ♡K lead. It will also give you nearly 0.2 extra tricks per deal at matchpoints, a substantial difference (perhaps half a top every five deals). Why is the heart lead such a disappointment? It's because your six-card length suggests that either declarer or the dummy will be short in hearts.

How do you rate doubleton leads? You will hear players speak of them in condescending terms. The truth is that they are much better than is generally thought. Leading from two spot cards is particularly effective. The aim is not to score a ruff in the suit; indeed, this will happen relatively rarely. The main purpose is to lead towards whatever honors partner may hold in the suit.

When you are declarer, you will often lead from a holding such as ♣75 in your hand towards ♣KQ83 in the dummy. You aim to establish a trick or two in clubs. The effect can be just the same if you are defending and lead from ♣75 against some suit contract, despite the fact that you have no idea what partner holds in the suit. Occasionally, you will find partner with the ♣AK, or the ♣AQ over dummy's ♣K, and he can give you a third-round ruff. Very much more often, you will begin the process of setting up one or more tricks from his honor holding. It may be essential to lead *towards* these cards, rather than leaving partner to lead away from them.

The bidding is 1♠–3♠–4♠. What will you lead from this hand?

♠ A 10 6 2   ♡ 8 5 3 2   ◇ 6 4 3   ♣ 9 8

A trump lead would clearly be foolish. Which side-suit lead is best? You should lead from the shortest suit, choosing the ♣9. Look at it this way. Suppose you strike lucky and find partner with KQJ7 in the suit that you lead. He is likely to enjoy more winners, before declarer ruffs, when you are short in the suit. If you lead a heart, hitting partner's ♡KQJ7, declarer will hold a doubleton (perhaps even a singleton) in either his hand or the dummy.

Leading a trump

There are two main situations where a trump lead is likely to be effective in a constructive sense. The first is when responder has left the opener in his second (probably shorter) suit:

West	North	East	South
			1♠
pass	1NT	pass	2◇
pass	pass	pass	

What deductions can you make when North passes 2◇? If he holds, say, two spades and three diamonds, he will usually give preference to 2♠ (particularly at matchpoints, where a successful spade partial would score more). It is, therefore, quite possible that responder holds only one spade and three diamonds. You should nearly always lead a trump on this type of auction, aiming to reduce the number of ruffs that declarer can take in the dummy. Look also for auctions like this:

West	North	East	South
			1◇
dbl	pass	pass	pass

East has passed your takeout double for penalties. He will have (or at any rate *should* have) a fairly solid trump holding, such as ◇KQJ98. Your intention should be to draw declarer's low trumps before he can score too many ruffs in his hand. You should lead a trump, even if you hold only a singleton, which is quite likely on this bidding.

Listen to the bidding

Suppose the bidding has gone:

West	North	East	South
			1♠
2◇	2♡	pass	2♠
pass	4♠	all pass	

What would you lead from this hand:

♠ 8 2   ♡ A K   ◇ Q J 10 6 5 2   ♣ K J 10

Leading from an ace-king is everyone's idea of a sensible thing to do. Not here, though! Dummy has bid hearts and it will be declarer's job to set up that suit. You should lead one of the unbid suits. It is too dangerous to lead from a KJ10 combination. You should lead the ◇Q, even though you have a six-card suit and it is likely to be ruffed by declarer at an early stage.

A simulation shows that a diamond lead has a 25% chance of beating the contract and a top heart only an 18% chance. The diamond lead is easily best at matchpoints too.

Try this lead problem from the Swedish National Pairs:

West	North	East	South
			1◇
pass	1♡	pass	2◇
pass	3♣	pass	5◇
all pass			

What would you lead from:

♠ A Q 9 6 4   ♡ 6 4 2   ◇ 10 4   ♣ J 4 2

When the opponents shy away from a possible 3NT (particularly at matchpoints), you should nearly always lead the unbid suit against five of a minor. Several West players duly led the ♠A and received an encouraging signal from partner. A second spade was played to East's ♠K, and the defenders had found the only way to hold declarer to +600.

Leading against a suit slam

Nearly all textbooks advocate passive leads against 6NT, because the opponents are likely to hold a high point count. They go on to advocate aggressive opening leads against suit slams. This is much more contentious. Suppose the opponents have bid to 6♠. (Yes, a particular auction may help you to choose your lead. We are looking, in general terms, at the types of lead that tend to work well.) What would you lead from this hand?

♠ 2   ♡ J 7 5 3   ◇ 10 8 7 2   ♣ K J 9 2

During the three decades or so before I started to run computer simulations, I would have been delighted to lead the ♣2. It is the worst lead of the four! It is worst whether or not you think the present opponents might bid a slam with two top club losers. At both IMPs and matchpoints, you should lead one of the red suits, with a diamond having a narrow edge.

The odds for an aggressive lead improve when you hold two touching honors. Let's say that the opponents reach 6♠ and you are on lead with:

♠ 9 3   ♡ Q J 8 4   ◇ Q 6 5   ♣ K 10 7 2

At both IMPs and matchpoints, the ♡Q is best (followed closely by a trump). The ♣2 is way behind in last place.

For decades players have asked, 'Should I lead an ace against a slam?' Back in the mists of time, a happy-go-lucky attitude was taken to slam bidding. Many slams were bid where the defenders could cash two top tricks in a side suit, and ace leads were consequently quite popular. Nowadays, most serious players will check that each suit is controlled, by using control-bids (formerly known as cuebids). There is much less chance that an ace lead will be rewarded by a cashable king in partner's hand. Consequently, leading an ace is not so popular.

This applies only at IMPs! Computer simulation has shown that it is often essential to cash a side-suit ace against a widely bid matchpoint slam; otherwise, you will often allow declarer to score an overtrick in a slam that was unbeatable anyway. Suppose the opponents bid to 6♡ at matchpoints, on some auction or other. What would you lead from:

♠ 10 8 4 3   ♡ 9   ◇ A Q 7 2   ♣ 10 6 5 2?

The prospects of an ◇A lead at IMPs vary according to whether the auction convinces you that the opponents have confirmed that they hold a control in each of the side suits. What can be said for certain is that the ◇A is *easily the best lead at matchpoints*. It is best by the massive margin of 0.3 tricks per deal! (This is the case when, so far as you can judge, a good number of pairs will bid the slam.)

Leading against an obvious sacrifice

Suppose you are West, holding:

♠ 9 5   ♡ Q 9 7 2   ◇ A Q 2   ♣ K 8 6 5

Your partner opens 1♡ and South overcalls 1♠. You bid constructively to 4♡, following your chosen methods, and the opponents sacrifice in 4♠, which you or your partner doubles. What should you lead?

Some players will say, 'Your side has the majority of the points. Declarer's only chance to do well is to score lots of trump tricks. Lead a trump!' Computer simulation does not back this analysis. On the assumption that you would have made 4♡, the target (particularly critical at matchpoints) will vary between down two and down four, depending on the vulnerability. Whatever the target may be, you do best to lead the ♡2, rather than a trump. On a heart lead, your expectation of defensive tricks is 5.9 per deal, compared with 5.7 on a trump lead. The extra trick that you score on one deal in five may be worth more than half a top.

SUMMARY

- A side-suit singleton is one of the very best leads you can make against a suit contract. Low doubletons (such as ♡85) also make excellent leads — not so much to score a ruff, but because you may be leading towards partner's honors.

- Leads away from an honor or two non-touching honors are likely to give away a trick and are not generally recommended. Such leads may strike gold at IMPs, where your sole aim is to beat the contract. At matchpoints, they are more likely to give away an extra trick. Remember that most game contracts cannot be defeated on any lead.

- The widespread recommendation to make an aggressive lead against a suit slam is overstated. Particularly at matchpoints, you should be wary of leading from a queen and very wary of leading from a king.

- When you hold an ace against a matchpoint suit slam, you should consider leading it. The chance that this trick will go away if you lead some other suit is much higher than most people think. This advice applies mainly at matchpoints, when you think that the slam will be widely bid.

TE$\int$T YOUR$\int$EL$\int$

1. (a) ♠ J 4 2   (b) ♠ A 10   (c) ♠ 5 4
        ♡ A 2   ♡ J 8 7 6 4 3   ♡ K J 9 4
        ◇ K 9   ◇ J 10 9 8   ◇ K 10 2
        ♣ 10 9 8 6 4 2   ♣ A   ♣ J 8 6 4

The bidding is 1♠–3♠–4♠. What will you lead from each of these hands? Would it make any difference if it was IMPs or matchpoints?

2. (a) ♠ A 7   (b) ♠ 10 5   (c) ♠ 4
        ♡ Q J 10 9 4   ♡ 10 9 8 5   ♡ A 5
        ◇ 10 5   ◇ Q J   ◇ 10 9 8 7 4 2
        ♣ 10 9 8 4   ♣ K Q 9 7 5   ♣ Q J 5 3

The bidding is 1♠–4♠. What will you lead from each of these hands? Would it make any difference if it was IMPs or matchpoints?

3. (a) ♠ 8 3 2   (b) ♠ 9 7 3   (c) ♠ —
        ♡ 2   ♡ Q   ♡ 8 5 4
        ◇ J 8 6 4 3   ◇ K Q J 8 7 6   ◇ J 9 3 2
        ♣ A 10 4 2   ♣ 8 6 3   ♣ A J 10 9 5 3

Respectable opponents bid to 6♠ on an auction that convinces you that they will not be missing a cashable ace and king in one of the side suits. What will you lead from each of these hands? Would it make any difference if it were IMPs or matchpoints?

ANSWERS

1. From (a) the ♡A is easily best at both IMPs and matchpoints. If a continuation seems unattractive when dummy appears and you see partner's signal, you may wish to switch to the ◊K. The ♡A gives you a 30% chance of beating the contract, against 24% for the ◊K. A club lead, perhaps the choice of many players, offers only a 21% chance, although it is second best, behind the ♡A, at matchpoints.

   From (b) the ♣A is easily best. It will beat the contract 58% of the time. (The ♠A is next best, with a 44% chance.) The ♣A gives you a huge 0.3 tricks per deal advantage at matchpoints too.

   Leading from a king in (c) is not a good idea. The result is a near tie between a trump and the ♣4. Remember that leading from a jack is fairly safe, almost as safe as leading from spot cards. A trump lead may save declarer a queen-guess in the suit, but the chance of this happening is only around 2%.

2. On (a) the eye is attracted to the heart sequence. It would be a good lead at notrump, yes, but the five-card length suggests that declarer will ruff at an early stage. Easily best is the ◊10 from a doubleton (at both IMPs and matchpoints). The general purpose of such leads is to establish honors in partner's hand. Here, the chance of an eventual diamond ruff is enhanced by you holding the ♠A.

   On hand (b) the ◊Q from a doubleton wins comfortably, with the ♣K in second place.

   Hand (c) completes a hat-trick of wins for the previously maligned doubleton leads. The ♡A finishes ahead of the ♣Q.

3. On (a) you should not lead your singleton against a suit slam when you hold an ace. It's very unlikely that partner holds an entry to give you a ruff! The ◊4 is the best prospect at IMPs, but at matchpoints you should bank your ♣A. By doing so, you will score a fifth of a trick more per deal than you can expect after a diamond lead.

   On (b) the singleton ♡Q lead will beat the slam 26% of the time. The handsome-looking ◊K lead will beat the slam only 8% of the time! In general, six-card suits do not make good leads. Declarer is very likely to hold a singleton in one hand or the other, particularly in a slam. The ♡Q is best at matchpoints, too.

   On hand (c) the ♣A gives you a 24% chance of beating the slam; your hope is that partner will hold a singleton club. A passive heart lead gives only an 18% chance. Leading the ♣A gives you a huge 0.35 tricks per deal advantage at matchpoints.

23

CASHING OUT AT MATCHPOINTS

When defending, you often reach the point where declarer has set up some discards and it is essential that you immediately grab whatever tricks you can. This is particularly important at matchpoints, even if you cannot beat the contract. It is a painful experience to see declarer discard losers in a suit where you had the chance to score a top card or two.

Take the East cards on this deal:

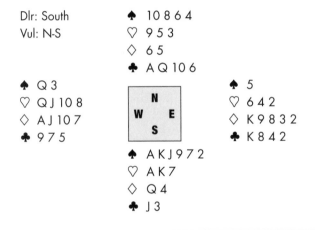

Dlr: South		♠ 10 8 6 4	
Vul: N-S		♡ 9 5 3	
		◇ 6 5	
		♣ A Q 10 6	

♠ Q 3   ♠ 5
♡ Q J 10 8   ♡ 6 4 2
◇ A J 10 7   ◇ K 9 8 3 2
♣ 9 7 5   ♣ K 8 4 2

          ♠ A K J 9 7 2
          ♡ A K 7
          ◇ Q 4
          ♣ J 3

West	North	East	South
			1♠
pass	2♠	pass	4♠
all pass			

West leads the ♡Q and declarer wins with the ♡A. He plays the ace and king of trumps, partner's ♠Q falling on the second round. Declarer's next move is to run the ♣J to your ♣K. How will you continue the defense?

You can be sure that in an average club game, some Easts would 'continue partner's suit', returning a heart. Declarer would win with the ♡K and discard two red-suit losers on dummy's surplus club winners, making an overtrick.

How can you work out what to do in the East seat? Declarer has six trump tricks. You know from partner's ♡Q lead that South also holds the ♡AK. Dummy's ♣AQ10 brings his total to eleven. If you return a heart, he will make those eleven tricks! It is essential to cash immediately whatever diamond tricks you can.

To make it easy for partner, you should play the ◇K and continue with the ◇3. You cannot beat the contract on this occasion, but you can prevent declarer from scoring an overtrick. This may be the eventual matchpoint table for the board:

N-S	E-W	Contract	By	Tricks	N-S score	E-W score	N-S MPs	E-W MPs
1	5	4♠	S	10	620		2	5
2	4	4♠	S	10	620		2	5
3	7	4♠	S	10	620		2	5
4	1	4♠	S	11	650		6	1
5	6	4♠	S	10	620		2	5
6	3	4♠	S	11	650		6	1
7	8	4♠	S	11	650		6	1
8	2	4♠	S	10	620		2	5

Stop declarer from making an overtrick and you score 5 MPs instead of 1 MP, a huge difference.

You are still East here, but you will have to defend with more subtlety:

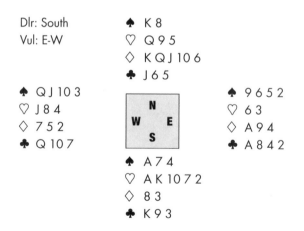

Dlr: South
Vul: E-W

```
                    ♠ K 8
                    ♡ Q 9 5
                    ◇ K Q J 10 6
                    ♣ J 6 5
  ♠ Q J 10 3                      ♠ 9 6 5 2
  ♡ J 8 4          N              ♡ 6 3
  ◇ 7 5 2      W       E          ◇ A 9 4
  ♣ Q 10 7         S              ♣ A 8 4 2
                    ♠ A 7 4
                    ♡ A K 10 7 2
                    ◇ 8 3
                    ♣ K 9 3
```

West	North	East	South
			1♡
pass	2◇	pass	2NT (12-14)
pass	4♡	all pass	

Your partner leads the ♠Q. Declarer wins with the ♠A and draws trumps in three rounds. When he plays the ◇4, your partner signals his length with the ◇2 (showing three cards in the suit). How will you defend?

There is little to be gained by holding up the ◇A, since declarer has a spade entry to the dummy. You win with the ◇A, noting that declarer has five trump tricks, two spade tricks and now four diamond tricks. You can see what will happen if you play ace and another club at this stage. Declarer will win the second round with the ♣K and cross to dummy to discard his last club.

You should lead a low club instead. This presents declarer with a guess in the club suit. If you hold the ♣A, yes, he could rise with the ♣K and discard both his remaining clubs to score two overtricks. He is hardly likely to do that, though, since he might then lose *three* club tricks and go one down. He will surely guarantee the contract by playing a low club from his hand. After all, this play will give him the overtrick that he seeks if you hold the ♣Q. The defense will then score two club tricks, holding declarer to +420 for an excellent E-W matchpoint score. Leading a low club instead of the ace will make no difference if partner holds the ♣K or the ♣KQ. It is likely to gain a trick when partner holds the ♣Q.

Cashing out against a high-level contract

At both matchpoints and IMPs, there is a useful method to help you cash your top tricks. Look at the situation faced by West on this deal:

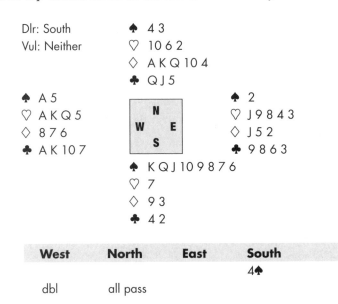

West	North	East	South
			4♠
dbl	all pass		

You lead a top heart from the West hand and dummy goes down with potential discards available on the diamond suit. You now need to cash a total of at least three tricks in hearts and clubs; your ♠A will then put the contract one down. If you guess incorrectly which cards to cash, and declarer ruffs the second round of hearts or clubs, he may be able to throw a loser away on the diamonds.

A recommended leading method against a contract at the game-level or higher is to lead the king from ace-king when you would like a count signal. On this deal you lead the ♡K. Partner's count signal of the ♡3 proclaims an odd number of hearts. Since this might be five, it is not safe to play another top heart. Instead, you switch to the ♣K, again asking for a count signal. Partner plays the ♣9, showing an even number of clubs. You now know that the ♣A will not be ruffed. You cash this card and the contract then goes one down. A potential disaster has been averted.

The lead of an ace requests an attitude signal (*ace for attitude, king for count*). At the five-level or higher, nearly all pairs play that an ace lead denies the king. On that basis, partner would encourage with the king but not with the queen. At the four-level or lower, it is reasonable to assume that an ace lead is from the ace-king, and you should encourage or discourage accordingly.

SUMMARY

- By counting declarer's tricks, you can often tell that you must cash the defenders' winners immediately. Otherwise, declarer will discard one or more losers in those suits.

- Against contracts at the game-level or higher, lead the king from ace-king to ask for a count signal. An ace lead asks for an attitude signal and will deny the king when the contract is at the five-level or higher.

TEST YOURSELF

1.

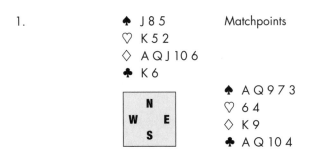

♠ J 8 5
♡ K 5 2
◇ A Q J 10 6
♣ K 6

Matchpoints

	N	
W		E
	S	

♠ A Q 9 7 3
♡ 6 4
◇ K 9
♣ A Q 10 4

West	North	East	South
		1♠	2♡
pass	4♡	all pass	

Your partner, West, leads the ♠2 against the heart game. You win with the ♠A and return the ♠7, declarer winning with the ♠K, as partner follows with the ♠6. After playing the ace and queen of trumps, your partner following, declarer leads the ◇3 to the ◇Q (partner showing count with the ◇2). What is your plan for the defense?

2.

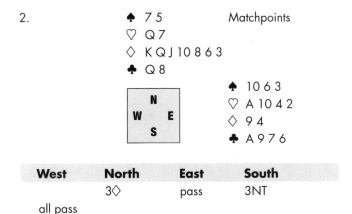

♠ 7 5
♡ Q 7
◇ K Q J 10 8 6 3
♣ Q 8

Matchpoints

	N	
W		E
	S	

♠ 10 6 3
♡ A 10 4 2
◇ 9 4
♣ A 9 7 6

West	North	East	South
	3◇	pass	3NT
all pass			

Your partner, West, leads the ♠Q against 3NT. Declarer wins with the ♠A, and plays the ♣3 to the ♣Q (West following with the ♣5). How will you defend?

ANSWERS

1.

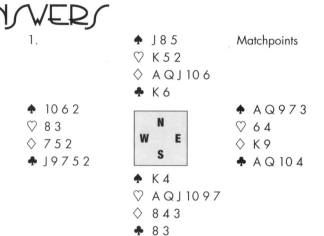

♠ J 8 5
♡ K 5 2
◇ A Q J 10 6
♣ K 6

♠ 10 6 2
♡ 8 3
◇ 7 5 2
♣ J 9 7 5 2

♠ A Q 9 7 3
♡ 6 4
◇ K 9
♣ A Q 10 4

♠ K 4
♡ A Q J 10 9 7
◇ 8 4 3
♣ 8 3

Matchpoints

Against 4♡, partner leads the ♠2 to your ♠A. Declarer wins your ♠7 return and draws trumps with the ace and queen, continuing with a low diamond to the queen. You win with the ◇K and count declarer's tricks. He has six trump tricks, one spade already made and four diamond tricks. That is a total of eleven if you defend passively by returning the ♠Q. No, you must cash the ♣A! Otherwise, declarer will score an overtrick for a very good matchpoint score. Your partner could have beaten the contract with an impossible-to-find club lead. That is no reason to lose concentration and fail to take the available tricks after some different lead.

2.

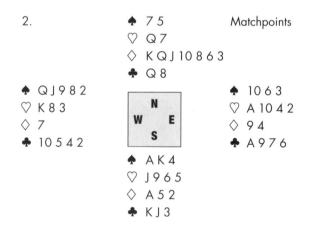

♠ 7 5
♡ Q 7
◇ K Q J 10 8 6 3
♣ Q 8

♠ Q J 9 8 2
♡ K 8 3
◇ 7
♣ 10 5 4 2

♠ 10 6 3
♡ A 10 4 2
◇ 9 4
♣ A 9 7 6

♠ A K 4
♡ J 9 6 5
◇ A 5 2
♣ K J 3

Matchpoints

West leads the ♠Q against 3NT. Declarer wins with the ♠A and plays a club to the queen and your ace. Declarer surely holds the ◇A. If you return a spade, he will score two spades, seven diamonds and some number of clubs. To reduce the overtricks you should play the ♡A and another heart now.

24

Forcing Declarer to Guess

You will know, from the many deals that you have played as declarer, how happy you are to be given a peaceful time. You like to be able to take one chance to make the contract and then fall back on another if the first chance fails.

When you are defending you must do your best to hustle the declarer! You must try to mislead him, so that he thinks one line is working and will not have time to switch to another when he realizes what has happened.

You must also force him to make decisions before he is ready to do so. Suppose he wants to discover whether a suit is 3-3 and will provide a discard, before falling back on a king-finesse in a different suit. Perhaps you can lead through his ace-queen in the second suit before he knows how the first suit is breaking. Take the East cards on this deal:

```
Dlr: South          ♠ A K 3
Vul: N-S            ♡ Q J 7 3
                    ◇ Q J
                    ♣ A K J 7

♠ J 10 9 5                      ♠ 8 7 2
♡ 8 2              N            ♡ 5 4
◇ 10 7 5 4 3    W     E         ◇ K 9 8 6
♣ 9 6              S            ♣ Q 10 4 3

                    ♠ Q 6 4
                    ♡ A K 10 9 6
                    ◇ A 2
                    ♣ 8 5 2
```

West	North	East	South
			1♡
pass	2NT	pass	4♡
pass	4NT	pass	5♣
pass	6♡	all pass	

North's Jacoby 2NT shows at least a game raise and South's 4♡ indicates a minimum hand. North discovers three keycards opposite and bids 6♡.

Your partner leads the ♠J, dummy winning with the ♠K. Declarer draws trumps in two rounds and finesses the ♣J. What will you return when you win with the ♣Q?

Suppose you return a spade, not realizing that anything special is required of you. Declarer wins and tests the clubs, hoping that a 3-3 break will permit a diamond discard. When clubs are 4-2, he will fall back on his second chance — running the ◇Q. His luck changes and he makes the contract.

What can you do about it? When you win with the club queen, you should switch to the ◇9! Declarer then has to decide whether to finesse in diamonds or to rise with the diamond ace and rely on a 3-3 club break (or a minor-suit squeeze on West, finding him with four clubs and the ◇K). Given the opportunity, he may well guess wrong and go down. Note that you play the ◇9, a high spot card, to give the impression that you do not hold the ◇K.

Pretending that declarer's first plan has worked

Sometimes you can make declarer think that his first chance has succeeded.

```
Dlr: South        ♠ K 8 5
Vul: E-W          ♡ K Q 5 4
                  ◇ K Q 9 2
                  ♣ A 3

♠ 9 7 6                      ♠ 10 3 2
♡ 10 9 8          N          ♡ 7 3 2
◇ 10 8 6      W       E      ◇ A J 5
♣ 9 8 4 2         S          ♣ Q 10 7 6

                  ♠ A Q J 4
                  ♡ A J 6
                  ◇ 7 4 3
                  ♣ K J 5
```

West	North	East	South
			1NT
pass	6NT	all pass	

You are sitting East and partner leads the ♡10 against the 6NT. Declarer has ten tricks on top, and a certain eleventh trick to come from the diamonds. What chances does he have for a twelfth trick?

There are two possibilities. If West holds the ◇A, declarer could make two diamond tricks by leading towards the ◇KQ twice. The other chance is that a finesse of the ♣J may succeed.

Let's say that declarer wins the heart lead with the jack and leads a diamond to the king. Sitting East, what is your plan for the defense? Suppose you win with the ace and return one of the major suits. Declarer now knows that he will score only one diamond trick. He will eventually steel himself to take the club finesse and make the slam when the ♣J wins.

By taking the ◇A on the first round, you make life easy for declarer. Indeed, you force him into the winning line. It is better to allow the ◇K to win, following nonchalantly with a low card as if you did not hold the ace. What will declarer do now? He will have to guess whether to play a second round of diamonds towards the queen or to take the club finesse. If you managed to find a smooth duck on the first round of diamonds, there is a very good chance that he will rely on the ◇A being well placed. Enjoy the moment as you score the ace and jack of diamonds!

> **THINK ABOUT...**
>
> *Suppose North was the declarer on this hand and you could not see his ◇KQ. You would still need to duck the ◇A on the first round to give you a chance of beating the slam. It would be clear, both from the bidding and the play, that declarer was very likely to hold both diamond honors.*

On the next deal you can play on declarer's desire for overtricks. Take the West cards here:

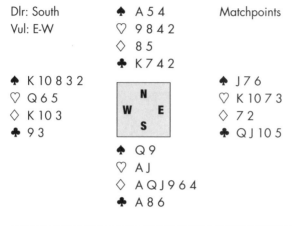

Dlr: South	♠ A 5 4		Matchpoints
Vul: E-W	♡ 9 8 4 2		
	◇ 8 5		
	♣ K 7 4 2		

♠ K 10 8 3 2
♡ Q 6 5
◇ K 10 3
♣ 9 3

♠ J 7 6
♡ K 10 7 3
◇ 7 2
♣ Q J 10 5

♠ Q 9
♡ A J
◇ A Q J 9 6 4
♣ A 8 6

West	North	East	South
			1◇
pass	1♡	pass	3NT
all pass			

It's not the best lead as the cards lie, but you start with the ♠3, East's ♠J forcing South's ♠Q. Declarer crosses to the ♣K and leads a diamond to the queen. How will you defend?

If you win with the ◇K, declarer will score ten tricks for 430. The bidding suggests that South has powerful diamonds, and you duck smoothly. Declarer has seven top tricks now. If diamonds are 3-2, he can bump this to ten tricks by continuing with the ace and another diamond. Still, if that's the case, why not cross to the ♠A and repeat the diamond finesse? Six tricks from the diamond suit will give him a handsome 460.

There is a fair chance that declarer will follow such a line. When you win with the ◇K, you can score three spade winners, holding declarer to 400. If you'd won the ◇K at Trick 2, declarer would have scored ten tricks for 430.

Playing the card you are known to hold

Many players go through their whole playing careers without realizing that they are greatly assisting declarer in situations where they could have put him to a difficult guess:

Dlr: South
Vul: E-W

	♠ A 7 3	Matchpoints
	♡ 9 7 3 2	
	◇ K J 4	
	♣ K J 6	

♠ Q J 10 8 2
♡ K 5
◇ Q 10 7
♣ 8 4 2

```
     N
  W     E
     S
```

♠ 9 6
♡ Q J 10 8
◇ 8 5 3
♣ 10 9 7 5

♠ K 5 4
♡ A 6 4
◇ A 9 6 2
♣ A Q 3

West	North	East	South
			1NT
pass	3NT	all pass	

North very reasonably elects not to bid Stayman with his 3=4=3=3 shape and a weak heart suit. Sitting West, you lead the ♠Q. Declarer wins with the ♠K and finesses the ◇J. When it wins, he has nine top tricks and the contract is safe. His thoughts will turn towards a possible overtrick.

Declarer continues with the ◇K, and the key moment of the hand is reached. Suppose you play on autopilot, following with the ◇10. When declarer leads the ◇3 on the next round and your partner produces the ◇8, he will rise with the ◇A. Because the earlier finesse of the ◇J won, he knows that you hold the ◇Q! He will score four diamond tricks for the great matchpoint score of +430.

To give declarer a losing option, you must drop the ◇Q under dummy's ◇K. You are **playing the card you are known to hold**. It costs nothing because the ◇Q and ◇10 are equal cards once the ◇J has been played. If declarer assumes that you began with a doubleton ◇Q, he will finesse the ◇9 next, losing to the ◇10. You will restrict him to +400, scoring well yourselves.

SUMMARY

• You can sometimes force declarer to take an early view on a suit. By switching through an AQ tenace, for example, you may force him to guess whether to finesse the queen before he has a chance to test some other suit.

• When declarer leads towards a king-queen combination and you are sitting in fourth seat with the ace, it is often beneficial to duck smoothly on the first round. Declarer may then be tempted to lead towards the queen subsequently, hoping that your partner holds the ace.

• Similarly, it may work well to hold up when declarer finesses with AQJ in the dummy and you hold the king in fourth seat.

Teſt Yourſelf

1. Dlr: South
    Vul: E-W

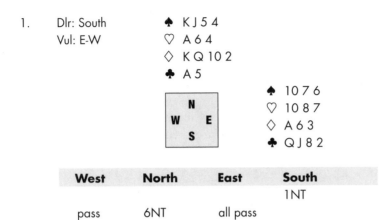

♠ K J 5 4
♡ A 6 4
◇ K Q 10 2
♣ A 5

♠ 10 7 6
♡ 10 8 7
◇ A 6 3
♣ Q J 8 2

West	North	East	South
			1NT
pass	6NT	all pass	

Your partner, West, leads the ♠9 against 6NT. Declarer wins in his hand with the ♠A and leads low to the ◇K. What is your plan for the defense?

2. Dlr: South
    Vul: Neither

♠ 7 5 2
♡ 6 4 3
◇ K 7 6 2
♣ A 8 3

♠ 9 8 4
♡ A K J
◇ Q J 10 8
♣ 7 6 4

West	North	East	South
			1♡
pass	2♡	pass	4♡
all pass			

You lead the ◇Q against 4♡ and declarer wins with dummy's ◇K, your partner playing the ◇3. Declarer then leads dummy's ♡3. Partner plays the ♡7 and declarer the ♡10. What is your plan for the defense?

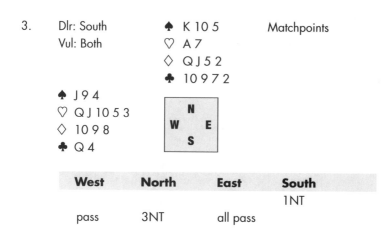

3. Dlr: South   ♠ K 10 5   Matchpoints
    Vul: Both   ♡ A 7
    ◇ Q J 5 2
    ♣ 10 9 7 2

♠ J 9 4
♡ Q J 10 5 3
◇ 10 9 8
♣ Q 4

West	North	East	South
			1NT
pass	3NT	all pass	

You lead the ♡Q against 3NT. Declarer wins in his hand with the ♡K and leads low to the ♠10. Your partner wins with the ♠A and returns the ♡8 to dummy's ace. Do you foresee any possibility to make life difficult for declarer?

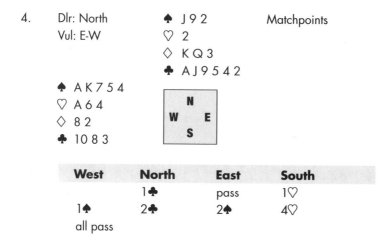

4. Dlr: North   ♠ J 9 2   Matchpoints
    Vul: E-W   ♡ 2
    ◇ K Q 3
    ♣ A J 9 5 4 2

♠ A K 7 5 4
♡ A 6 4
◇ 8 2
♣ 10 8 3

West	North	East	South
	1♣	pass	1♡
1♠	2♣	2♠	4♡
all pass			

You play three rounds of spades, South ruffing the third round. Declarer reaches dummy with the ◇K and leads a trump. East plays the jack and declarer the king. What is your plan for the defense?

ANSWERS

1.

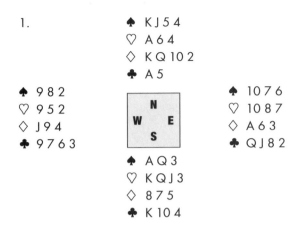

Defending 6NT, partner leads the ♠9. South wins with the ♠A and leads a diamond to the king. Declarer surely needs a few diamond tricks to make the slam. If West holds the ◇J, you have a chance. You must follow smoothly with a low card on the first diamond. This will put declarer to a guess in the suit. When he subsequently leads a second round of diamonds, he will have to guess whether to play the ◇Q or the ◇10. If he chooses to play the ◇Q, the defense will score two diamond tricks for one down.

2.

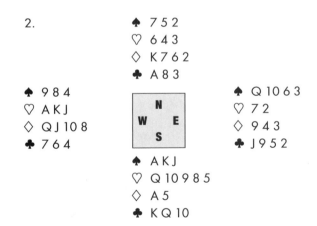

Sitting West, you lead the ◇Q against 4♡. Declarer wins with dummy's ◇K and leads low to the ♡10. Suppose you win with the ♡J and persevere with diamonds. Knowing that he has three trump losers, declarer will play trumps from his hand and eventually use the ♣A to take a successful spade finesse. Instead, you should win the ♡10 with the ♡K! Now, declarer may be tempted to use the ♣A to repeat the trump finesse.

3.

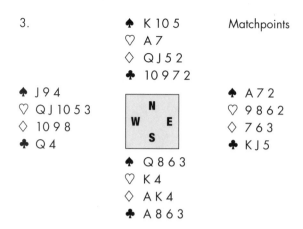

♠ K 10 5
♡ A 7
◇ Q J 5 2
♣ 10 9 7 2

Matchpoints

♠ J 9 4
♡ Q J 10 5 3
◇ 10 9 8
♣ Q 4

♠ A 7 2
♡ 9 8 6 2
◇ 7 6 3
♣ K J 5

♠ Q 8 6 3
♡ K 4
◇ A K 4
♣ A 8 6 3

You lead the ♡Q against 3NT. Declarer wins with the ♡K and tries a spade to the ♠10. This draws the ♠A, and he has nine top tricks. Partner clears hearts and declarer then plays dummy's ♠K. If you play the ♠9, he will know that you still hold the ♠J; he will play to the ♠Q on the third round and score a precious overtrick. Instead, you should drop the ♠J on the second round. Declarer may then be tempted to try for an overtrick by finessing the ♠8. You will cash three hearts to defeat the contract!

4.

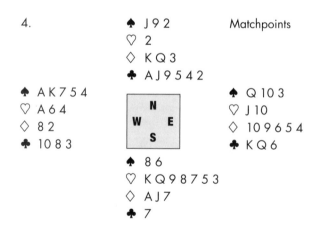

♠ J 9 2
♡ 2
◇ K Q 3
♣ A J 9 5 4 2

Matchpoints

♠ A K 7 5 4
♡ A 6 4
◇ 8 2
♣ 10 8 3

♠ Q 10 3
♡ J 10
◇ 10 9 6 5 4
♣ K Q 6

♠ 8 6
♡ K Q 9 8 7 5 3
◇ A J 7
♣ 7

You play three rounds of spades against 4♡, declarer ruffing the third round. He crosses to the ◇K and leads a heart to the jack and the king. If declarer has an eight-card trump suit, the game is easily his. You must hope that declarer holds only seven trumps, and that your partner has the ♡Q or ♡10 alongside the ♡J that he has just played. Defeat of the contract is certain if partner holds the ♡Q. If he holds the ♡10, you must duck smoothly on the first round of trumps. Declarer is then likely to play East for ♡AJ, leading the ♡9 on the next round. (This is the correct play, by Restricted Choice.) He will then lose two trump tricks and go one down.

Master Point Press on the Internet

www.masterpointpress.com

Our main site, with information about our books and software, reviews and more.

www.teachbridge.com

Our site for bridge teachers and students — free downloadable support material for our books, helpful articles and more.

www.bridgeblogging.com

Read and comment on regular articles from MPP authors and other bridge notables.

www.ebooksbridge.com

Purchase downloadable electronic versions of MPP books and software.